P9-APE-025

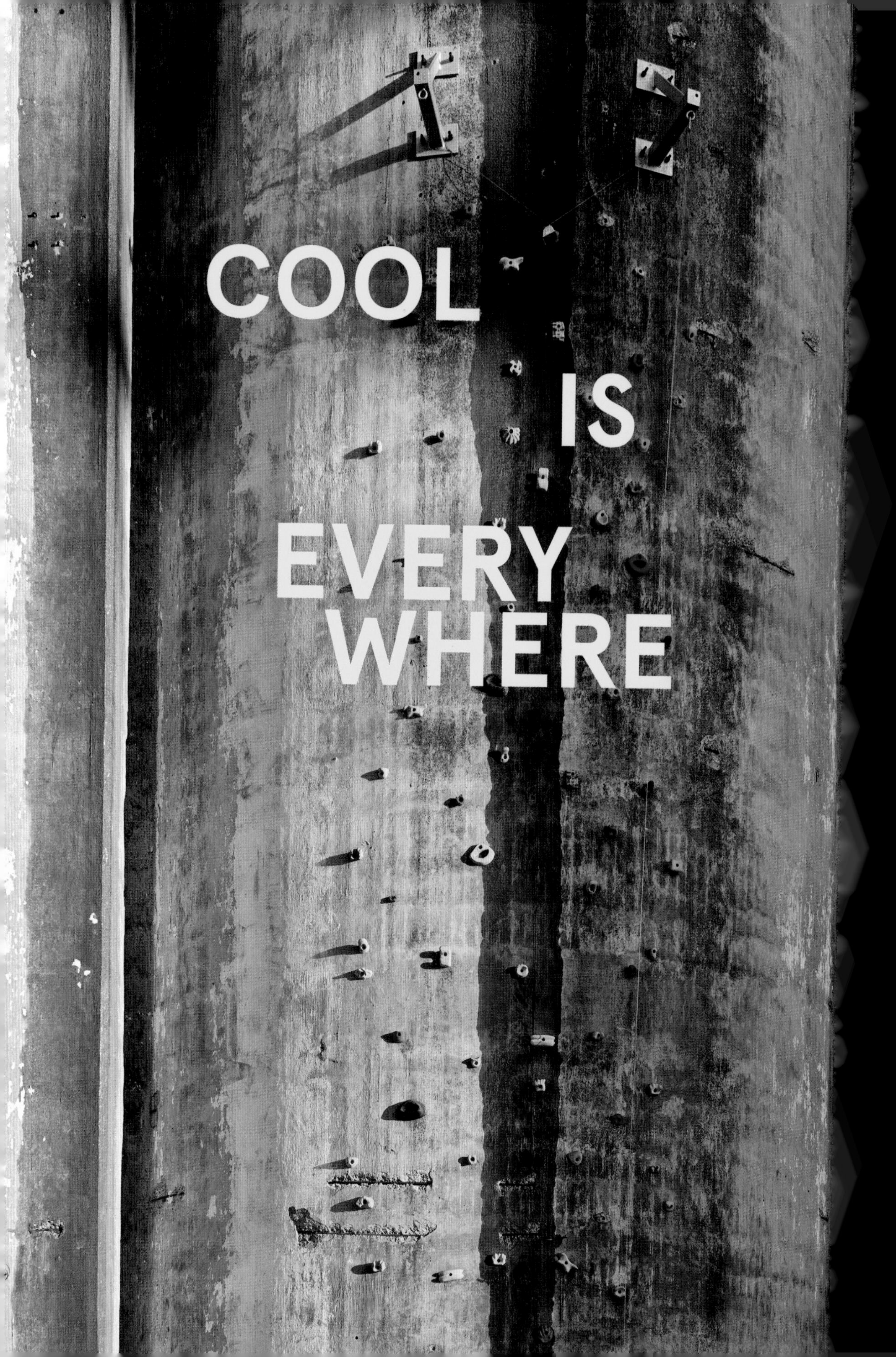
COOL
IS
EVERY
WHERE

IS
WHERE

NEW AND ADAPTIVE DESIGN
ACROSS AMERICA

MICHEL ARNAUD

INTRODUCTION BY DONALD ALBRECHT

TEXT WITH JANE CREECH

ABRAMS, NEW YORK

CONTENTS

ON THE ROAD TO CHANGE

BY MICHEL ARNAUD

Work on this book started right as I was finishing my book, *Detroit: The Dream Is Now*. My wife, Jane, our son, Will, and I would drive out to Detroit from our loft in New York City, and often we would stop in Pittsburgh. Detroit had been an eye-opener on how cities can change—how old buildings could find new life and purposes, like becoming an artist studio or an art gallery; how a new museum could change a city block; how people were craving green spaces; and how a coffee shop, a brewery, or an interesting food scene would lead to the creation of a boutique hotel. Jane and I found these changes in Pittsburgh, of course. We began to notice these signs of change on other trips as well, and in our own backyard. Jane grew up in Greenville, South Carolina, and with each visit we would hear about a new restaurant or art gallery or learn about a new neighborhood. While on vacation, we had lunch at The Grey in Savannah—the restaurant was once a Greyhound bus station—and dinner at the Kitchen Sync in Greenville—in what was once a dairy, or ice cream shop. Art dealer Jack Shainman turned an empty elementary school into a branch of his cutting-edge New York City gallery, with museum-quality exhibitions in Kinderhook, New York, 20 minutes from our house in upstate New York. While on a magazine assignment, I met designer Rob Feinstein. We spent part of the day together and he invited our family to visit his home in Asbury Park, New Jersey. We took the kids to the beach, walked along the boardwalk, and ate at Porta, a pizza restaurant in a former industrial building that had been the Student Prince bar back in the day. During the course of lunch, we talked about the changes Asbury Park was going through after years of decline. We talked about Detroit and its evolving scene. We talked about what it was like to live outside New York City, how urban life was

spreading to smaller towns. At one point, Rob said, "Yes, cool is everywhere," and that became the working title for this book. After that, Jane and I started to investigate other cities. We put together a list of 14 midsize cities with populations under a million. My fascination with postindustrial cities inspired our process. We looked at towns that had suffered a downturn and were now celebrating a comeback. We looked to the design media who were reporting on cities, such as *Architectural Digest*, *Architectural Record*, and *Design Milk*. We pulled out the map, which made us look to the West Coast and the Midwest. We talked to friends with connections to cities we were interested in, for example, architect and artist Rajiv Fernandez, whose mother, Maria, had an Indian restaurant in Omaha, Nebraska, for 40 years; architect Evan Watts, whose family has deep ties to Birmingham, Alabama; and curator Ingrid Schaffner, who grew up in Pittsburgh and recently returned. We hit the "road" with our four-year-old son in tow, grouping our travels by locale. While we spent three to four days in some cities, such as Portland, Oregon, we returned again and again to others—Greenville, South Carolina; Pittsburgh, Pennsylvania; North Adams, Massachusetts; and Oakland, California. We would book appointments in advance for projects we wanted to see, but at the same time, we left the door open for serendipity and discovery. There were occasions when one person would say, "Oh, you have to see this," or we would be driving down a street and I'd stop the car to jump out with the camera. As the book took shape, architecture and design curator Donald Albrecht was organizing an exhibition of adaptive reuse projects in New York City titled *Authenticity and Innovation* for the Center for Architecture. We had breakfast to discuss the introduction of the book and he in turn introduced us to friends and colleagues such as Barbara Campagna in Buffalo, Jeanne Giordano in Portland, Bridget Gayle Ground and Cathy Henderson in Austin, and Darrin Alfred in Denver. As momentum was gathering in our research process, we felt it reflected the movement we experienced as we crossed the country and spoke to artists, designers, architects, homeowners, and businesspeople.

How did we define *cool*? Webster's defines it as something excellent or hip. We found it to be at the intersection of old and new, when a project is strikingly new in an old place, or when something changes the context that we see it or experience it in. Somehow when you see something cool, you know it. As we traveled, people would tell us about their projects, how they came to be, the impetus and the ideas that inspired them, and their process in order to get to the finished results you will find on these pages. They talked about what it was like to work with an old building, with the special challenges of taking an old structure into the present or integrating a new building in an old neighborhood. We heard about the design choices that were made, from making sure a building was structurally sound to deciding what to leave and what to modernize. We were impressed with the creativity, manual labor, and just plain hard work that went in to each one of these places. People also talked about their concerns for the growth in their cities with a mix of excitement and trepidation—"It's great to have a restaurant in the neighborhood, finally" or "What will these changes mean . . . more traffic? How will the rising home prices affect the value of my home? Will I be able to afford to live there?"

Over the course of the project, we were in the process of leaving our home in New York City. It was a small loft in a 19th-century textile building in Tribeca—Jane had lived there for almost 30 years. A developer bought the building for redevelopment. While we realized how lucky we were to leave on our own terms, we also experienced how painful and heartbreaking it can be to move on. It seems ironic that the people who pioneer a neighborhood can't always live there as long as they want. What became clear over the course of working on this book and our move is that change is the nature of cities. And as big cities move to

The dining room of the Detroit Foundation Hotel— a former fire department building was converted into a boutique hotel in 2017.

accommodate the luxury market, smaller cities are incorporating elements of an alternative urban lifestyle—walkable neighborhoods, green spaces, and cultural communities—with surprising and refreshing results.

Photographing urban spaces has its own challenges. Early in my career, I worked as a reportage photographer working for newspapers and magazines such as *Vogue* and *Harper's Bazaar* covering fashion shows, among other subjects. In later years, interior photography became my new love: It's all about light, composition, and atmosphere. This project called on both areas of visual expression: the spontaneity of reportage and the reflective nature of interior photography.

Is "cool" everywhere? The question is certainly open-ended. I hope this book will modestly elicit a positive answer: Yes, cool is everywhere. You just need to be curious enough to look around and discover the signs of new sensibilities and attitudes that are reinventing the past to create a present full of possibilities and opportunities— another window on the American Dream.

SUNNY-SIDE CITIES

BY DONALD ALBRECHT

Coolness is everywhere, all across the United States, in cities large and small. One barometer of urban hipness, "36 Hours," the *New York Times* series exploring what to do when you have that many hours in a city identifies coolness in chic boutiques, craft breweries, and cultural venues from museums to art galleries. *Condé Nast Traveler* magazine announces the must-go-to eateries that make a metropolis an "official" food city, while the publishers of the Wallpaper City Guides compile curated checklists of where the savvy traveler needs to go when venturing to one of their anointed cool cities.

Within the cache of cities covered by these bibles of cool, there is a new urban phenomenon: the rise of midsize or "secondary" cities that were formerly held in low esteem but that have recently experienced new life. Attracting not only culinary and cultural tourists, these cities are luring new residents as well. Their upswing reflects dramatic demographic shifts across America. While during the first part of the 2010s people concentrated in big cities and large metropolitan areas, more recently they are leaving the nation's supercities—New York, Los Angeles, San Francisco, and Chicago—often in favor of smaller cities. Today, Nashville, Sacramento, Tampa, and Austin are among the top-10 American cities in terms of the in-migration of new residents.

No longer looked down upon as backwaters, America's formerly secondary cities are attracting people for a variety of reasons. Many midsize cities now provide the high-quality culture and cuisine associated with big cities, without the latter's hassles, overcrowding, and traffic congestion. They also offer easier access to outdoor recreational opportunities, with spectacular landscapes for hiking, biking, and a range of sports. And today's midsize cities are safer than they have been in decades.

Like the downtowns of their larger counterparts, their business districts long stood empty and were perceived to be dangerous. How were people convinced to come back downtown? To cite one example, "Birmingham needed to relearn how to come downtown," says Cheryl Morgan, emerita professor and director of the Auburn University Urban Studio, about the Alabama city she calls home, "and the programming of the city's new 19-acre Railroad Park, and then a new baseball park—provided that initial hook. When they came they found it safe—not the reputation of downtown; beautiful; interesting; and worth coming back to."[1]

While all these factors play a role, however, the revitalization of midsize cities rests on strong economic underpinnings. Midsize cities offer more affordable housing and lower costs of living than larger cities. They attract young workers because their city governments try hard to diversify their economies; Denver, for example, is today a city "on the sunny side of the American economy," according to the *New York Times*. It's home to a wide range of businesses, including technology start-ups and financial service firms—a far cry from the 1980s, when, in the words of one city official, it was focused on "Coors, carbon and the Cold War."[2] Local business and civic leaders in smaller cities are actively seeking ways to lure all-important high-tech jobs in particular. They are aided in their efforts by numerous foundations and businesspeople. Former America Online CEO Steve Case, for example, created the Rise of the Rest Seed Fund, which tries to convince Silicon Valley firms to consider setting up shop in cities such as Nashville and Columbus, Ohio. The presence and expansion of major research universities also enliven the economies of cities from Pittsburgh, home of Carnegie Mellon, among other

The Hotel Henry Urban Resort Conference Center on the Richardson Olmsted Campus in Buffalo, New York, opened in a former mental asylum.

highly regarded schools, to Buffalo, where the University at Buffalo, the State University of New York, recently opened a center for genome research. And recent tax changes, capping state and local deductions at $10,000, disproportionately affect residents of larger cities, located in states with high property taxes, making smaller cities in the South and Midwest even more attractive.

Whether they are locals who decide to stay in or return to smaller cities, or those leaving the big city for the first time, today's entrepreneurs often take advantage of the opportunities available in smaller communities by opening up art galleries, breweries, and shops. They become part of what sociologist Eric Klinenberg calls a town's "social infrastructure." While public institutions, such as libraries and schools, and community organizations like churches compose the most common definition of a city's social infrastructure, commercial places like cafés and bookstores, which fellow sociologist Ray Oldenburg terms "third spaces," are also important generators of social capital. Such places, in Klinenberg's words, are ones

"where people are welcome to congregate and linger regardless of whether they've purchased. Entrepreneurs typically start these kinds of businesses because they want to generate income. But in the process . . . they help produce the material foundations for social life."[3]

The vibrancy of today's smaller cities rests not only on broad cultural and economic factors but also on three particular features not previously considered to be important components of a compelling urbanism: the preservation of historic buildings and places, the reclamation of degraded landscapes, and the fostering of small-scale industries described by city dwellers as "maker culture."

ARCHITECTURE

Throughout the country, the residents of smaller cities and towns are rethinking their historic architecture, particularly in their decaying downtowns, and repurposing it. Monumental urban buildings, though suitable for their time, became obsolete in the mid-20th century. Train travel declined after World War II with the rise of the interstate and air

An empty bank in Greenville, South Carolina's Village of West Greenville
is now home to a design studio and shop.

travel, people moved from cities to suburbs, and manufacturing moved offshore. In the 1950s, '60s, and '70s, many old buildings were destroyed and only a few people like urbanist Jane Jacobs warned of the negative consequences of their destruction. "Old ideas can sometimes use new buildings," she proclaimed. "New ideas must use old buildings."[4]

In time, the pervasive postwar "new-is-always-better" attitude gave way. Though Jacobs and other civic leaders fought to save Penn Station in New York in the mid-1960s and lost, their efforts helped solidify the movement to put in place laws to save buildings and districts. These efforts were aided in the 1970s by federal tax credits that encouraged private-sector investment in rehabbing and reusing historic buildings, allowing developers to deduct 20 percent of many improvement expenses from their tax liability. More recently, states have offered developers of historic properties an additional 20 percent.

To progressive urban thinkers, old buildings embody cultural memory and moor rapidly transforming cityscapes as they are continually reshaped by development pressures and evolving architectural taste. Adaptive reuse projects across the country—old department stores transformed into stylish hotels, bus stations into innovative restaurants, schools into cutting-edge galleries—prove that a city's residents can build their futures upon older structures. "Architecture is important," notes Mick Cornett, four-term mayor of a revived Oklahoma City, Oklahoma. "New investment will need something to build from."[5] And old buildings can be major contributors to what sociologist Richard Florida calls "quality of place." "Authenticity—as in *real* buildings, *real* people, *real* history—is key," he notes, citing cities like Providence, Rhode Island. "A place that's full of chain stores, chain restaurants, and chain nightclubs is seen as inauthentic. Not only do those venues look pretty much the same everywhere, but they also offer the same experiences you could have anywhere."[6]

The search for authenticity in the form of old buildings drives millennials, the large and diverse generation born between about 1981 and 1996 that is a magnet for marketers. A recent survey commissioned by American Express and the National Trust for Historic Preservation, for example, found that 97 percent of millennials value historic preservation. Forty-four percent want to live in neighborhoods with historic buildings, 52 percent prefer shopping in historic city centers, and when traveling, 67 percent opt to stay in historic hotels.[7]

What makes all of this possible is that the range of historic buildings in midsize cities is as rich and diverse as it is in their big-city counterparts. The Industrial Revolution of the 19th century, the Gilded Age after the Civil War, and the Jazz Age economic boom of the 1920s sparked the construction of magnificent structures, from an art deco train station in Omaha, to a high-end department store outside Cincinnati. Today, these buildings have been revitalized and now provide places for people to live, work, and play. Greenville, South Carolina, is a prime example of a city making use of its historical architecture to evolve. It was a textile-manufacturing town and has gone through innumerable boom-and-bust cycles. Its architectural legacy—great masonry textile mills and their ancillary buildings—has remained largely constant, however, for more than 150 years. Now those buildings are key to the city's revival. The massive Romanesque Revival Mills Mill was built in 1896 and has recently been converted to loft-style condominiums.

Frequently, the adaptive reuse of old buildings manifests the transformation of the American economy from one based on manufacturing to one focused on service and accommodates industries that were in their infancy or not even conceived when these structures were built. In Portland, Oregon, an old awning factory now houses Swift, an advertising and marketing agency, while Buffalo's old Niagara Machine and Tool Works factory is being retrofitted into the 100,000-square-foot Northland Workforce Training Center. Housing classrooms and industrial shops and labs, the center will be a place where people will learn the skills to work in advanced manufacturing and electric utility industries. Northland will serve the local workforce, and not the cultural tourists who flock to the city's rich historic sites, such as the Hotel Henry Urban Resort Conference Center, formerly H. H. Richardson's magnificent late 19th-century

Buffalo State Asylum for the Insane. As a result, Northland will "help the city to become more equitable," according to Buffalo architect Barbara Campagna, who is working on the project.[8]

Vying for tourist dollars and cultural cachet, midsize cities often turn to the arts. Omaha's train station has functioned as the Durham Museum, dedicated to the history of the region and also offering a range of traveling exhibitions since 1996.[9] Earlier that decade, Nashville-based businessman Thomas F. Frist Jr. and his family came to realize that their city's largely abandoned main post office was an ideal candidate for Nashville's first major art museum. The mid-1930s art deco building's vast central sorting room is shielded from natural illumination, making it perfect for a gallery in which to display light-sensitive art. Completed through a public-private venture between the Frist Foundation, the city, and the US Postal Service, the Frist Art Museum opened in 2001.

New museums also spark new urban development. Benefiting from its proximity to such cultural magnets as Williams College, the Clark Art Institute, and the Norman Rockwell Museum in the Berkshires region of Massachusetts, the town of North Adams strode onto the cultural landscape with the opening of the MASS MoCA contemporary art center in 1999. Located on the site of the former Sprague Electric Company, the project resulted from the city seeking ways to reuse the recently closed plant and the aspiration on the part of the staff of the Williams College Museum of Art to find spaces large enough to accommodate art that was too big for traditional galleries.

Hotels and restaurants followed in MASS MoCA's wake, and today North Adams is home to the emerging Greylock WORKS, a 240,000-square-foot mixed-use facility on a nine-acre campus that comprises a dramatic event space offering farm-to-table tastings, conferences, community gatherings, and design markets as well as hosting weddings and other private events. There are also professional co-working spaces, artisanal food and beverage production facilities, with loft condominiums and a locally sourced restaurant in the offing. The project is being developed and designed by architects Salvatore Perry and Karla

Rothstein, principals in the New York City–based LATENT Productions. They had encountered the immense neglected site—initially a fine-cotton-spinning mill, built in 1870, and subsequently an aluminum-processing plant—in 2014. After a year of due-diligence research, they purchased the property. The city's strong advocacy of the project allowed the Greylock WORKS's team to compete for grants from state and federal programs. Perry's and Rothstein's investments have reaped rewards for the community. The project aims to foster "agri-tourism" and support local farmers. Further helping the local economy, Perry and Rothstein created their own general contracting company in Massachusetts. Throughout the project's evolution, engaging the community has brought, in Perry's words, "the benefit of optimism."[10]

RECLAIMED LANDSCAPES

Successful midsize cities are reclaiming not only their old buildings, but also whole derelict landscapes. Like their counterparts in big metropolitan areas, civic leaders and entrepreneurs in smaller cities are realizing that people need to enjoy time in nature as a counterbalance to long hours spent in air-conditioned offices and homes, often in front of computer screens.

In these cities, the residue of industrial and transportation infrastructures is being revived into innovative landscapes combining new sports, recreation, and entertainment destinations that serve as gathering places. These new spaces often retain elements of their former grittier selves, yet another marker of today's interest in the authenticity of old, "real" places. In Denver, old bridges have been reclaimed and integrated into paths for pedestrians and cyclists, while Birmingham's Railroad Park has helped revitalize the entire city. Located on a former warehouse and brick-making site and using materials recovered from it, the park was discussed for several decades but gained a real sense of possibility with the support of numerous city actors, from the nonprofit advocacy group Operation New Birmingham, which sought to understand what the city collectively valued—one answer was green space—to Mayor Bernard Kincaid, who attended a meeting organized by

the Mayors' Institute on City Design, which convinced him to move the park forward. Opened in 2010, the park today brims with family activities, concerts, cultural events, and opportunities to watch the trains that pass nearby. The park also boosted civic spirit. "The completion of Railroad Park—its beauty, excellent design, and the way it was embraced by the city," says Cheryl Morgan, "brought out in our city an almost overwhelming sense—for the first time in a long time—of success. A 'we can do it!' sense. And we can do first class."[11] Making landscapes like this one all the more alluring is that accessing them often proves easier to do in smaller cities than in larger stretched-out ones where distances are greater and clogged roads more numerous.

One of the most creative of these new landscapes is Buffalo's RiverWorks, the city's first privately funded waterfront tourist facility, located along the Buffalo River on a former industrial strip. Combining hockey rinks, a roller-derby track, concert facilities, and restaurants, among venues for other purposes, RiverWorks also reuses the site's cylindrical grain elevators, which famous modernist architects from Walter Gropius to Le Corbusier had celebrated as industrial masterpieces. Six of these elevators have been painted blue to resemble a six-pack of Labatt Blue beer, sponsor of a local hockey tournament. Plans call for other elevators to house a brewery and distillery.

MAKER CULTURE

America's great modern cities arose in the early 20th century from economies based on corporate enterprise. Wall Street banks forged New York, automakers created Detroit, and movie companies made Los Angeles. Today, at the start of the 21st century, corporations like Google and Amazon certainly play major roles in urban formation, but they often do so alongside small-scale entrepreneurial businesses that enhance a midsize city's quality of life. Participants in this maker culture include artists and artisans, many of whom were the urban pioneers who moved into old, abandoned downtowns in search of affordable space and spurred those downtowns' revival. Makers also include purveyors of craft beers and artisanal coffees, and owners

The tailor's shop of Ledbury, a luxury men's clothing company, is in an old department store in downtown Richmond, Virginia.

of small shops and galleries offering individually selected goods that, like Greenville's Art & Light Gallery, promise "curating life is our passion."[12]

Today's urban entrepreneurs start and run their own businesses as physical expressions of their personal identities. Consider Denver's Michael M. Moore, who founded Tres Birds Workshop in 2000. The workshop offers its clients both design and hands-on building services and focuses on the adaptive reuse of old buildings, recycling their historic materials to conserve resources. Tres Birds has turned wood bowling alley lanes into conference tables and wood flooring into framing for skylights. Tres Birds's Denver projects include STEAM on the Platte, a 3.2-acre mixed-use development comprising workspace for tech companies; the Family Jones Spirit House, a distillery; and a building at 2601 Larimer, which houses the restaurant Il Posto. The latter building is located in RiNo, or River North, a former industrial hub just north of downtown that has taken shape over the

last 20 years and is now a dense neighborhood of youth-oriented creative businesses. RiNo's creative pulse manifests itself in streetscapes adorned with huge hand-painted murals. Moore was one of their early painters and today sits on the board of CRUSH, a nonprofit that raises funds from local developers to sponsor a fall festival of in-situ mural painting.

As Moore's story attests, small entrepreneurs can have a large impact on the cities in which they live. Artist Diane Kilgore Condon, for example, bought the old general store built for the people who worked in Greenville's Brandon Mill, a few miles west of downtown, and converted it into an art gallery and artists' studio called ArtBomb Studio. By 2014, ArtBomb was putting on special events that not only attracted hundreds of people but also helped launch new galleries, studios, and restaurants that revived the whole area. Similarly, artist and developer Sarita Waite and her husband, University of California, Berkeley, architecture professor Raymond Lifchez, created North Oakland's

Temescal Alleys, two pedestrian ways that comprise locally owned artisan shops and a café.

Admittedly, such small places often represent the exclusive end of the marketplace. The Ledbury Workshop in Richmond, Virginia, for example, employs workers making the company's bespoke line of shirts, which begin at $265. "Companies will bifurcate their product lines," Ledbury CEO Paul Trible has noted. "Uniform-volume product will be made abroad, and highly personal, customizable goods will be created domestically. Our customers can choose from a ready-to-wear shirt made in Turkey, a made-to-measure shirt made in Poland or a truly bespoke shirt made in Virginia."[13]

THE FUTURE OF THE MIDSIZE CITY

The advent of highly specialized, high-end manufacturing in midsize cities such as Richmond speaks volumes about large demographic shifts nationwide and raises a large question: Will such cities be victims of their own success? Will their revival spark the high housing prices, overdevelopment, and traffic congestion that big cities face, the absence of which made the midsize city so attractive in the first place? Evidence suggests that this is already happening in cities such as Denver. Rising housing prices are starting to push people out of the city, and the popularity of RiNo has prompted at least one of its pioneering developers to sell his property there and search for less well-trodden, grittier urban enclaves.

While today's newly growing midsize cities enjoy economic prosperity, they are struggling with the creeping conformity that it can bring. For example, Texas's state capital is seeking to live up to its commitment to "keep Austin weird" in the face of its high-tech status; Google recently announced they will soon occupy all 35 floors of a downtown office building. *BuzzFeed*'s Julie Gerstein, in an article titled "10 Underrated Cities that Hipsters Are About to Ruin," asked her readers, "Is your life a neverending stream of artisanal coffees and avocado toast?"[14]

In the realm of interior design, trendy food meets its match in the ubiquity of architectural signifiers of hipness—rough-hewn brick walls, recycled wood elements, and industrial lighting—in innumerable bars and restaurants. At the same time, international corporate hotel chains now create their own divisions of boutique hotels. Marriott-branded Autograph Collection Hotels, for example, includes the Hi-Lo Hotel, a conversion of the 1910 Oregon Pioneer Building, an office building in downtown Portland.

Midsize cities face larger urban challenges than cultural conformism. Their prosperity is not always equally shared by all of their residents. Historian and urban planner Alan Mallach states in his recent book *The Divided City: Poverty and Prosperity in Urban America* that in postindustrial metropolises, or what he calls "legacy cities," such as Pittsburgh and Baltimore, "the revival is ignoring the poor."[15] Neighborhoods like Pittsburgh's Lawrenceville and Baltimore's Canton and Hampden attract an affluent population, and new businesses flourish, while people living in poorer areas, often disproportionately African American, don't benefit. "From one legacy city to the next," Mallach writes, "as some areas gentrify, many other neighborhoods, including many that were pretty solid, relatively stable working-class or middle-class neighborhoods until fairly recently, are falling off a social and economic cliff."[16] And disparities also exist between midsize cities that now find themselves in a Darwinian struggle to succeed and attract new business. The *New York Times* recently identified a growing inequality among midsize cities. It noted that Nashville; Columbus, Ohio; and Indianapolis are "thriving because of luck, astute political choices and well-timed investments," while other cities such as Providence and Rochester, New York, are slipping.[17]

How midsize cities will address their challenges, both large and small, remains to be seen. Will they be able to retain their individuality and sense of authenticity? Can they preserve their distinctive urban fabrics and architecturally significant old buildings in the face of rising development? Will their art and craft makers be able to live in cities with rising rents? Will ethnic, racial, and economic diversity succumb to homogeneity? Only time will tell. In the meantime, the direction of midsize cities is upward; cool and thriving, they provide evidence of a new and vibrant American urbanism.

The Standard Elevator, on the Buffalo waterfront, was built in 1928 and was used as a flour mill.

ENDNOTES

1. Cheryl Morgan, in an email to the author, April 25, 2019.
2. Patricia Cohen, "The Cities on the Sunny Side of the American Economy," *New York Times*, March 31, 2016, accessed May 3, 2019.
3. Eric Klinenberg, *Palaces for the People: How Social Infrastructure Can Help Fight Inequality, Polarization, and the Decline of Civic Life* (New York: Crown Publishing Group, 2018), 16. Klinenberg cites Oldenburg's term "third spaces" on the same page.
4. Jane Jacobs, *The Death and Life of Great American Cities* (New York: Vintage Books, paperback edition, 1961), 188.
5. Mick Cornett with Jayson White, *The Next American City: The Big Promise of Our Midsize Metros* (New York: G. P. Putnam's Sons, 2018), 210.
6. Richard Florida, "What Draws Creative People. Quality of Place," *Urban Land*, October 11, 2012, accessed April 19, 2019.
7. These statistics appear in the press release, dated June 27, 2017, for the survey "Millennials and Historic Preservation: A Deep Dive into Attitudes and Values," authored by the National Trust for Historic Preservation, accessed May 13, 2019.
8. Barbara Campagna, in an interview with the author, May 1, 2019.
9. The museum opened as the Western Heritage Museum in 1996. It was renamed the Durham Western Heritage Museum in 1997 and the Durham Museum in 2008.
10. Salvatore Perry, in an interview with the author, May 10, 2019.
11. Cheryl Morgan, in an email to the author, April 25, 2019.
12. Art & Light Gallery website, accessed May 17, 2019.
13. Paul Trible, quoted in Ben Thompson, "Ledbury CEO: Workshops, not factories, are US manufacturing's future," CNBC, May 27, 2016, accessed May 21, 2019.
14. Julie Gerstein, "10 Underrated Cities that Hipsters Are About to Ruin," *BuzzFeed*, October 9, 2017, accessed May 17, 2019.
15. Alan Mallach, quoted from his book *The Divided City: Poverty and Prosperity in Urban America* (Washington, DC: Island Press, 2018) in Eillie Anzilotti, "American cities are reviving—but leaving the poor behind," *Fast Company*, July 5, 2018, accessed May 17, 2019.
16. Ibid.
17. Ben Casselman, "Nashville Leaves the Pack Behind," *New York Times*, December 17, 2018.

NORTH

MASSACHU

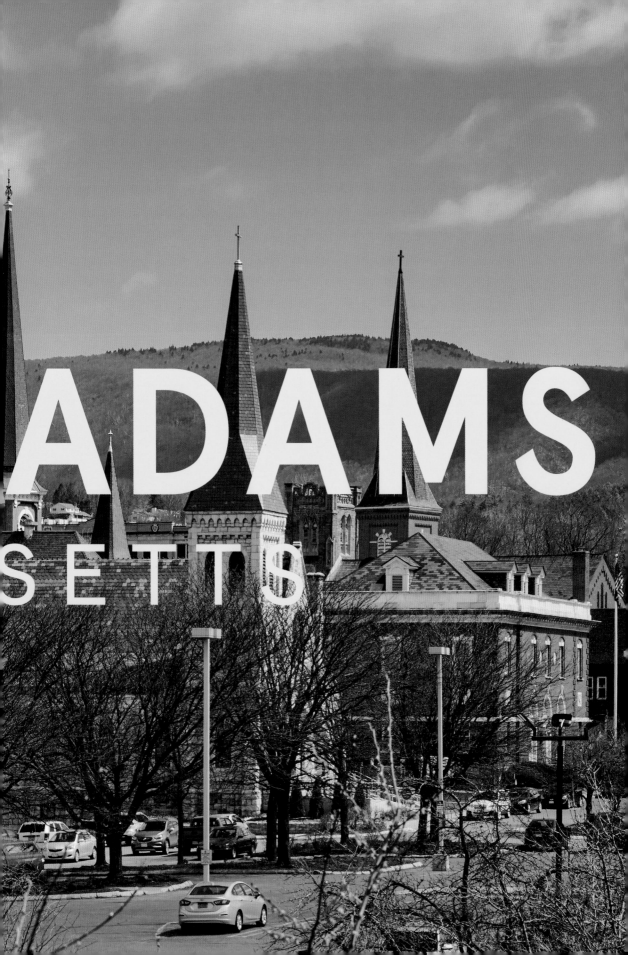

NORTH ADAMS, MASSACHUSETTS, IS LOCATED in the northwestern corner of the state—at the border of Vermont and New York, in the Berkshire Mountains. The city was named for American statesman Samuel Adams, who was governor from 1794 to 1797. Early on, local mills harnessed the power of two branches of the Hoosic River that converge there, and the town built up around this industrial activity. North Adams (which split from the town of Adams) became known as a site for manufacturing, which continued for around 150 years; textiles were made at the Arnold Print Works, and later the Sprague Electric Company employed over one-third of the city's residents making consumer electronics. As companies went bankrupt, moved, or closed due to overseas competition, the town fell into decline. In the 1980s, nearby Williams College officials were looking for a place to display large pieces of art. North Adams's mayor, John Barrett III, suggested the old textile mill turned electrical company at 87 Marshall Street as a site for art installations. At first, the plans for a museum were embraced by the state, who along with private donors provided funding for the renovation of the site and the creation of galleries inside the acres of old brick buildings. The new Massachusetts Museum of Contemporary Art (MASS MoCA) opened in 1999. Along with its neighbors, Williams College Museum of Art and the Clark Art Institute, the destination art center has changed the area's economy to cultural tourism. Recent developments have been using a similar model—transforming old mills, giving them contemporary purposes. While the effects of these changes are still being realized—there continues to be a high level of poverty in North Adams—the world-class art community, nestled in the bucolic landscape, has created a momentum that's hard to ignore and offers the small city of North Adams a third or fourth act.

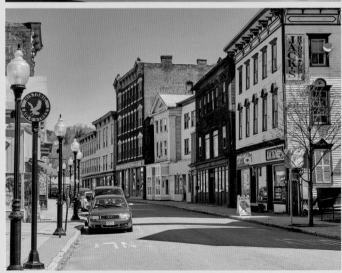

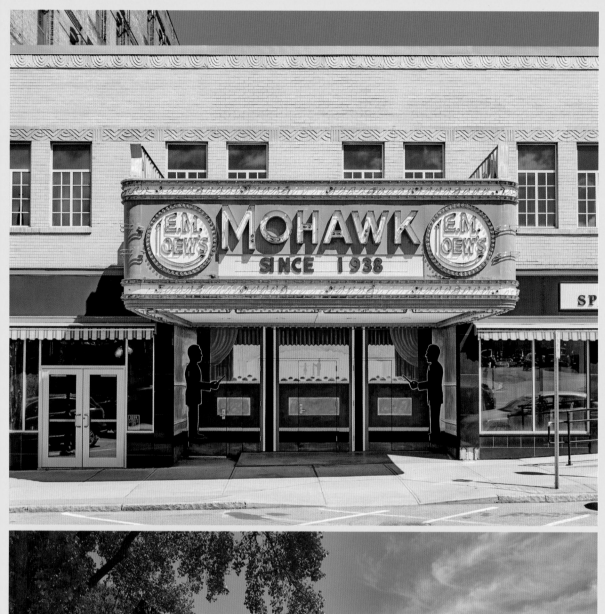

MASS MoCA

Massachusetts Museum of Contemporary Art (MASS MoCA) was the brainchild of North Adams mayor John Barrett III and Thomas Krens, former director of Williams College Museum of Art and later the Solomon R. Guggenheim Foundation. Krens was inspired by a visit to a Swiss textile mill that had been converted into an art museum. At first, Krens was looking for additional space for the Williams College Museum of Art exhibitions, but over the years the plans developed to turn MASS MoCA into an art center in its own right, with galleries, restaurants, and event spaces. The site needed extensive cleanup, renovations, and restoration, which were completed by the architectural firm Bruner/Cott & Associates. After years of fundraising and planning, the museum (led by director Joseph Thompson—who took the reins when Krens left for the Guggenheim) opened in 1999 with galleries and other wings to follow—the latest being Building 6, which opened in 2017. There are a total of 26 buildings—the earliest ones date to the 1860s—on the museum campus. Some galleries are connected by multiple passageways; others are freestanding structures. The museum is home to long-term installations by artists such as Jenny Holzer and Sol LeWitt.

ABOVE A steel railroad trestle from the site's previous life as a manufacturing facility remains a part of the museum's grounds.

ABOVE The entrance of MASS MoCA, with its brick facade and large-scale windows.

OPPOSITE *The Clocktower Project* (1999) by Christina Kubisch and Natalie Jeremijenko's *Tree Logic* (1999) are installed at the entrance of Massachusetts Museum of Contemporary Art in North Adams, Massachusetts.

One of the main museum buildings located along the Hoosic River. A series of bridges, both in the interiors and between structures, links the campus.

The new wing named Building 6: The Robert W. Wilson Building opened in 2017. The design of the new galleries was by Bruner/Cott & Associates.

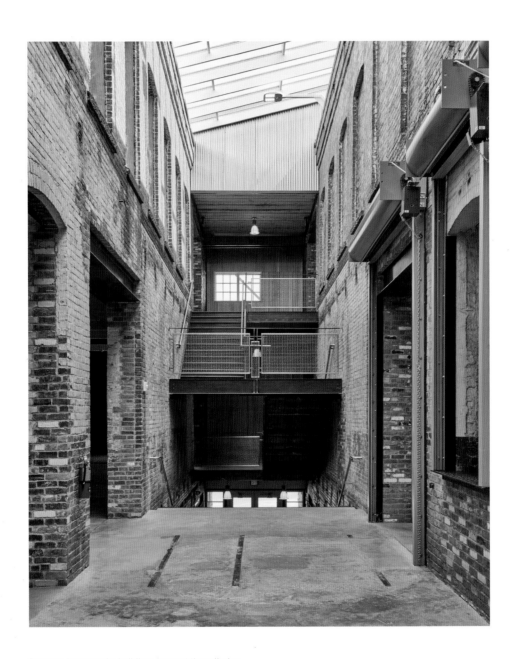

Passages between the buildings connect the galleries,
creating a continuous viewing experience. Some tunnels
are used as exhibition space for sound pieces.

GREYLOCK
WORKS

In 2015, architects Karla Rothstein and Salvatore Perry, who live in Brooklyn, bought the former Greylock Mill, which was part of the 19th-century textile industry in North Adams—approximately 240,000 square feet of space. They began an ongoing process of developing the site in phases to include an event center, studios, offices, a restaurant, a bar, and condominiums. While they were respectful of the existing features of the buildings—such as keeping the framework of the original windows where possible as well as the initial footprint, the renovation has been extensive and includes new elements. They also worked with TEND landscape to create a plan for terraces, a rain garden, and pathways surrounding and in harmony with the whole site.

ABOVE Rust of the remaining steel outbuildings known as the Butler Buildings has been worked into the aesthetic of the new structures added to the site, such as the ramps and entryways of the South Entry, which are made of weathering steel.

OPPOSITE The sawtooth roofline was preserved as part of the improvements to the original textile factory.

LEFT A view of the Greylock WORKS campus set against Mount Williams, a section of the Appalachian National Scenic Trail.

Other areas of the site are being prepared for redevelopment: the fourth floor of the Main Mill will be converted into loft apartments, and the old boiler room will be a bar one day.

ABOVE One of the first spaces to be transformed was the first-level weave shed of the mill, which is now used as the event center. The room, with its 14- to 25-foot ceilings, restored old-growth hardwood floors, natural light from the sawtooth roofline, and over 26,000 square feet of space, boasts a dance floor, a catering kitchen, and "industrial chic" bathrooms. Every summer Greylock WORKS hosts an artisanal food festival and market.

BELOW In the Engine House—a multipurpose room, there is a combination of surfaces, as seen in the old painted brick and new gypsum wallboard around the windows.

The Engine House contains a mixed-use space that shows the architects' intent to combine contemporary materials with those of the past. They installed a wall of floor-to-ceiling glass doors and windows while keeping the hinged Dutch doors of the surviving structure. The room has views of Mount Williams and Greylock to the south.

IN THE 1700S GREENVILLE, SOUTH CAROLINA, sat on the edge of the "frontier of the British Empire" according to historian Dr. Archie Vernon Huff Jr. Today, Greenville sits on the edge of a new kind of frontier that combines aspects of a sleepy Southern town with an astute business center and is held up as an example of the New South for its efforts to transform its downtown. Located between the megacities of Charlotte, North Carolina, and Atlanta, Georgia, and north of sophisticated Charleston, South Carolina, Greenville has worked hard to carve out its own identity that is connected to its place and history. Revitalizing the city started over 40 years ago as the textile industry, which moved to the city in 1860, left for Asia or went bankrupt. The intentional efforts of civic leaders and citizens to rethink the downtown—part new construction, part architectural preservations—also capitalized on the town's natural assets: the Reedy River, a temperate climate, and close proximity to the lakes and mountains of the Blue Ridge Mountain Range. Central to this development and its growth is the story about cycling. Former professional cyclist George Hincapie calls Greenville home and many of his followers and fans flock to the city to participate in his cycling rides. City planners took advantage of a federal Rails-to-Trails program to convert the Greenville and Northern Railway into the Greenville Health System Swamp Rabbit Trail. As the trail expands to other parts of the city, so does the development. Near downtown, the Village of West Greenville—once a mill village—has changed from vacant buildings to storefronts with new businesses, restaurants, nightlife, and an active art scene as well as offering new residences in the restored mill.

TERRY IWASKIW AND MELINDA LEHMAN RESIDENCE

A cycling trip brought consultant Melinda Lehman and her husband, designer Terry Iwaskiw, to Greenville. They had previously lived in major Northern metropolises, so when they decided to consolidate their lives and move south, they were looking for properties with personality and history. The former synagogue turned church was a great match for their collections and design sensibilities. Terry and Melinda are consummate collectors. Their home is filled with a highly selective combination of artworks and objects, some vintage, some contemporary. For example, a black plaque from a boys' and girls' school sits above a vintage optometrist's cabinet. A linocut of Bob Dylan is displayed over a vintage slot machine and reconditioned-steel shop cabinet. The master suite overlooks the main living area. On the ground level, the guest quarters are made up of two bedrooms and a sitting room and kitchenette. The couple worked with local architect, Trey Cole, on the renovations.

The couple decided to leave the signage of a church that occupied the building.
They did extensive renovations, which included adding a lap pool to the side yard.

TOP AND ABOVE The octagonal cupola and panel ceiling were restored. The library wall divides the kitchen, dining area, and the main sitting room from the office and media room as well as the bedroom upstairs. The half wall helps create an intimate setting in the large open room.

ABOVE Bedrooms are both upstairs and downstairs and are connected by a steel staircase.

The kitchen was designed as a room within a room. Its glass skylight and glass window walls made of chicken-wire panes and metal frames allow natural light in and through the space. A long counter made of honed Carrara marble is perfect for parties as well as breakfast coffee. A vintage surgical lamp was installed over the modern kitchen island's sink. The couple's collection of jadeite glass is displayed above the counters, which also showcase antique and contemporary kitchenware in green (naturally). All the major appliances and countertops are stainless steel.

THE ANCHORAGE

The Anchorage restaurant opened in January 2017 in the Village of West Greenville and is owned by Greenvillian Greg McPhee and his wife, Beth. Formerly the doctor's office for the Brandon Mill just down the street, the building was in bad shape. The couple took on the renovation project themselves, sourcing furniture and reconfiguring and expanding the kitchen. The restaurateurs opened up the front of the space by removing part of the second floor, creating a double-height ceiling. The entry includes a reclaimed church pew placed to accommodate those waiting for a table.

ABOVE Exposed bricks and beams as well as an open kitchen define the first-floor dining room.

MIDDLE Sunny Mullarkey McGowan and Elizabeth Kinney painted the mural of a bounty of fruits and vegetables on the outside of the building.

BELOW Owner/Chef Greg McPhee and his wife, Beth, stand in the main dining room of their restaurant.

ART & LIGHT GALLERY

In 2010, Teresa Roche, an artist and designer from Greenville, was looking for a new studio space when she came across a small house in the Village of West Greenville. It was the parsonage for the church across the street, built in 1947. She recognized its potential as a gallery as well as for shared studio spaces. A pioneer of the neighborhood, Art & Light is now one of 30 galleries and artist spaces in the growing arts district.

ABOVE Once the drop ceiling and the heavy drapes were removed, light flooded the rooms, says Roche. The walls and ceilings were stripped down to the original beadboard.

MIDDLE The modest parsonage-turned-gallery is located on a side street of the up-and-coming neighborhood.

BELOW "My family is a mill family and I've been in and out of this area since I was a child. I've always loved it and felt a connection to its charm and village feel," says gallery owner, Teresa Roche.

WEST VILLAGE LOFTS AT BRANDON MILL

The Brandon Mill, a cotton mill, opened in 1901 with 10,000 spindles and 400 looms. Over the years, other buildings were added to the campus, as was a baseball field, where the textile mills' employee teams competed against one another. The Brandon Mill team's most famous player was Shoeless Joe Jackson. The mill closed in the 1970s and the building was used as a warehouse, then offices, and now an apartment complex. The four-story red-brick building with its smokestack and water tower—all still intact—today sits on approximately 9.5 acres in West Greenville. Many of the mill village houses still survive and surround the building. At one time the mill supported a community of over 400 families.

TOP The water tank was preserved in the development of the complex.

RIGHT The lower level of the main mill was transformed into a wine cellar area for the residents. Part of the flooring of the second level has been removed to allow light into the spaces below and also to reveal the early-20th-century structural beams and brick columns.

OPPOSITE Like the water tank, the smokestack is original to the mill. The swimming pool was added when the building was renovated.

A two-story-high game room, with exposed brick walls and arched windows, is part of the shared space of the new apartment building.

ARTBOMB STUDIO

The ArtBomb Studio is a nonprofit art gallery and artists' studio. It was founded by artist Diane Kilgore Condon, who purchased the building—a former grocery store for the Brandon Mill—and opened the studio in 2001. Today, it contains the studios of 14 artists, including Kilgore. Public events are hosted by the resident artists. There is a gallery/lounge space in the front of the two-story brick building and a lush garden in the back.

OPPOSITE, ABOVE A painting on plywood by Paul Flint covered the broken front window.

OPPOSITE, BELOW Kilgore Condon opened up the ceiling in her studio to expose the original tin tiles.

ABOVE The everchanging facade of the ArtBomb Studio.

BELOW The gallery displays paintings by resident artists Paul Flint, Diane Kilgore Condon, and Katie Walker.

LEFT Painter Jo Carol Mitchell-Rogers's studio on the first floor.

ABOVE Diane Kilgore Condon created the garden in 2002, a year after the opening of the studio. The back garden was planted on a formal grid, but Diane Kilgore Condon decided to "let it go and be happy." Artists and friends have made donations in memory of loved ones. For example, the blue bottle tree was given in remembrance of Greenville neighbor Phil Dorn. Plants from the garden are used for events at the studio.

LOCATED ON THE WESTERN SHORE OF the state, at the confluence of the Erie Canal, Lake Erie, and the Buffalo River, Buffalo is the second-largest city in New York State, behind New York City. Given its geographical location, it became a center of transportation and for the production of steel and grain, eventually becoming one of the largest cities in America. Resources and dollars poured into Buffalo's development. Downtown has important buildings by architects such as Louis Sullivan, Daniel Burnham, and Louise Blanchard Bethune, one of America's first woman architects. The Albright Art Gallery (later to become the Albright-Knox Art Gallery) opened in 1905. Driving through the neighborhoods of Buffalo, which are linked by parkways, double-wide avenues lined with American elm trees, and traffic circles, you experience the planning of surveyor Joseph Ellicott and landscape architect Frederick Law Olmsted, who designed a multi-park system. Yet as transportation methods changed—becoming less dependent on shipping—the city felt a decline in the 1970s. Skip ahead to 2012, when New York State invested in its Buffalo Billion project, with plans to transform the Rust Belt city into a hub of revitalization. One of the new industries is solar power. While a few of the manufacturing plants still exist on the waterfront and continue to produce—for example, General Mills still makes Cheerios breakfast cereal there—most of the grain elevators have been abandoned and some are now being repurposed as breweries, parkland, and places for recreational activities. The housing stock built in Buffalo's heyday has largely remained. This remarkable infrastructure (and relatively low rents) is appealing to a new generation who are either returning home to Buffalo or who have attended University at Buffalo and wish to stay. The growth of the city is coming full circle—an expansion of the Albright-Knox Art Gallery by architectural firm OMA is planned for 2021.

DARWIN D. MARTIN HOUSE COMPLEX

Darwin D. Martin was an executive at the Larkin Soap Company in 1902 when he hired Frank Lloyd Wright to design his house—a compound of buildings including a home for his sister Delta and her husband, George Barton; a pergola; a carriage house/stable; a gardener's cottage; and a conservatory. After Martin died in 1935, the family moved out and the site was abandoned. A series of owners followed, and the main house was later used as the residence of the State University of New York at Buffalo's president. The site began its transformation into a museum when the Martin House Restoration Corporation was formed in 1992. The group was led by dedicated volunteers, including Mary Roberts, now its executive director. The corporation's mission is to restore the remaining buildings and reconstruct those that have been demolished—the conservatory, the carriage house/stable, and the pergola. The contemporary Eleanor and Wilson Greatbatch Pavilion—a visitor's center designed by Toshiko Mori—opened in 2009. The difference between the surrounding Victorian houses of the Parkside East Historic District and the Martin House brings the vision of Wright and Martin's passion into clear view.

ABOVE A view of the living room, looking toward the dining room. Wright designed many of the furnishings, but he also selected furniture for the home. The theme of nature permeated the overall design.

RIGHT The new visitor's center was designed by Toshiko Mori Architects.

OPPOSITE, TOP The Martin House is considered to be an example of Frank Lloyd Wright's early signature prairie style.

OPPOSITE, BOTTOM Looking through the pergola— a covered walkway—to the conservatory, where a reproduction of the Winged Victory is installed.

Wright designed details including the stained-glass windows and lighting fixtures, and the sconces in the library. The design of the window was named the *Tree of Life* and is seen throughout the house. The table was also designed by Wright.

BUFFALO RIVERWORKS

The Buffalo waterfront was and is the site of the city's innovative industrial activities. Even as the manufacturing has diminished there, there are still companies that have facilities along the Buffalo River and its canals. These days, the area is also being repurposed as venues for recreation and creativity. Partners Doug Swift, Earl Ketry, and John Williams opened the entertainment venue RiverWorks in 2015. They decided to preserve and incorporate the ruins of grain silos on the site into their project and create new facilities that include a restaurant, a brewery, an ice-skating rink, event spaces, and an indoor roller derby. The combinations and contrasts of old and new structures are striking and dramatic.

ABOVE The metal buffalo artwork (named "Tatonka") was a collaborative effort by Earl Ketry, Mark Madden, Tyler Griffis.

BELOW The circular remnants of the Grange League Federation grain elevators at RiverWorks are called "Stonehenge." The area has become a place for weddings and other events.

OPPOSITE Steel rebar from concrete pillars of demolished silos is reimagined as outdoor sculptures, known as *Medusa*, referring to the mythological character with snakes as hair. Steel hoppers from the abandoned grain elevators serve as a backdrop.

NORTHLAND WORKFORCE TRAINING CENTER

Funds from New York State's Buffalo Billions investment project were used to convert the former Niagara Machine & Tool Works, built in 1910, from an abandoned factory to a vibrant teaching center. Watts Architecture & Engineering and preservation architecture firm BAC/Architecture + Planning worked to incorporate existing elements, such as the skylights and sawtooth monitors, into the final design. The facility is over 100,000 square feet and provides space for classrooms, workshops, and labs along with administrative offices. Training focuses on energy-related manufacturing jobs.

LEFT The central lobby of the restored building was the original factory assembly shop that use to make stamping machines for manufacturing. The entrance features double-height windows, a yellow crane that dates to 1910, and skylights.

ABOVE The decision was made to keep the surface of the brick walls of the former factory. A three-dimensional mural created by students from the Society for the Advancement of Construction-Related Arts was installed against the masonry.

OPPOSITE The facade of the building features replacement windows, which were part of the restoration. The windows were chosen to match the original factory windows as closely as possible.

HOTEL HENRY URBAN RESORT CONFERENCE CENTER AT THE RICHARDSON OLMSTED CAMPUS

Early in his career, in the late 1800s, architect Henry Hobson Richardson was commissioned to design a state mental institution. Working with Dr. Thomas Story Kirkbride, who believed exposure to light, nature, and physical labor were key to recovery, Richardson designed central twin towers—known as the Administration Building—and opposing wings that form a massive necklace-shaped building. Frederick Law Olmsted's firm planned the complex's original campus. After the hospital closed in 1974, the "Richardsonian Romanesque" (as his style was called) buildings sat vacant for over 40 years. Plans to save the deteriorating structures, which were deemed a historic landmark and renamed the Richardson Olmsted Campus, were developed by preservationists, a private corporation, and New York State. In 2012, working with Flynn Battaglia Architects, Deborah Berke Partners was brought in to design the

first phase of the transformation of the Administration Building and two sections of the connected wings. Five years later, the campus opened the Hotel Henry Urban Resort Conference Center and 100 Acres: The Kitchens at Hotel Henry, a farm-to-table restaurant. The Berke team was considerate of the historic design, saving the wide corridors and guest rooms with soaring ceilings that reinforced Kirkbride's theories. However, significant—yet practical—contemporary updates, such as adding spacious bathrooms, were also needed. The most important addition was a spectacular steel and glass entrance at the back of the central Administration Building that changes the entry of the hotel and allows guests to arrive by car and have easy access to the restaurants and conference center. The transparency of the new entry's materials honors Richardson's vision—a fitting tribute to the past made present.

The hotel's suites are on the upper floors, where the wooden eaves have been incorporated into the new design.

Henry Hobson Richardson's master work, now known as the Richardson Olmstead Campus, was originally the Buffalo State Asylum for the Insane. The south entrance of the Administration Building features a new entry by Deborah Berke Partners.

Within the new glass addition is a staircase of glass, steel, and concrete that connects the back entry to the lower conference rooms and the original first floor of the building.

OPPOSITE The long corridors of the hotel lend themselves to the display of artists work such as this sculpture by Robert Then.

ABOVE The bar of 100 Acres: The Kitchens at Hotel Henry is on the first level.

BELOW An art piece, Shovelization Series by Denice Bizot hangs above the fireplace in the bar.

The graciously proportioned halls of the Hotel Henry's guest-room hallways were designed in 1880 for access to light and air. Deborah Berke Partners honored the original design and created meeting and sitting areas outside of the rooms as well as opportunities to showcase local artists' work. The dramatic rug was designed by the Berke team, as were the custom lighting fixtures.

THIN MAN BREWERY

Developer Rocco Termini converted a factory building on Chandler Street into the second location of the Thin Man Brewery. The building is also the second home of Tappo Pizza. The design of Benjamin Siegel of BMS Design Studio retained the industrial character of the interiors by stripping down the walls to their concrete pillars, exposing the ductwork on the concrete ceiling, installing a poured-cement floor, and keeping the garage-door openings. The large taproom is filled with artworks by Peter Cahlstadt. The graffiti style continues on to the beer garden outside. On-site beermaking takes place in the new building connected to the old factory.

OPPOSITE, ABOVE The taproom with its glass garage door has a bar with 16 taps as well as elevated tables for patrons.

ABOVE The second locations of both the Thin Man Brewery and Tappo Pizza is on Chandler Street in the Black Rock neighborhood.

OPPOSITE, FAR LEFT Light pours in from the large entry, where the Thin Man Brewery logo is painted on the wall.

OPPOSITE, LEFT Artwork by Mark Madden, titled *Art Channel 8*, covers the three-sided patio wall. Tables are set up, as are cornhole games.

THE CITY OF OAKLAND, CALIFORNIA, is located just over the Bay Bridge from San Francisco. Although many commute between San Francisco, San Jose, and Oakland, it is not a suburb but a city, with its own history, diverse population, and identity as an art-filled place (a 2014 *New York Times* article compared Oakland to Brooklyn as a center of artistic production). The city has been in the process of revitalizing since the 1990s, after the population had fallen over the previous 20 years and concerns over crime rose. Each of its neighborhoods have their own distinct character. For example, there is evidence of the city's robust past in the glamourous art deco-style buildings downtown. West Oakland has its share of warehouses that are now homes, offices, and studios for artists, makers, entrepreneurs, and start-ups. Walk down to water's edge through Jack London Square, passing by the restaurants and bars, to see shipping-container cranes, signs of an industry that made Oakland a commercial center. The 19 miles of the East Bay coast are not the only access to water important to the town. A saltwater lagoon, Lake Merritt, provides recreation and relaxation in the form of barbeque spots and running paths. Sitting in a café around the lake, there is the sense of a Mediterranean port city. On the hillside is a mix of traditional pink stucco and red ceramic tile-roofed houses with new and modern buildings. Together, each of these areas and their populations create a place filled with variety, where *e pluribus unum* comes to mind.

ABOVE AND OPPOSITE Metal containers for succulents welcome visitors and regulars off the street to the main bar and seating area for the café.

RIGHT The outside community table was placed parallel to the shipping container shop.

EQUATOR
COFFEES CAFÉ

The Equator Coffees café is in the walkable neighborhood of Adams Point, close to Lake Merritt. The historic area was once home to Auto Row, starting in the 1920s. The shop is made from a bright red recycled shipping container by UrbanBloc, a California design company. Also on the site—a former parking lot—are planters and a long "succulent table," made of Douglas fir and steel by Oakland artist Luigi Oldani. "You really get a California vibe when surrounded by succulents," says Equator's Director of Coffee Culture Devorah Freudiger.

CREATIVE GROWTH ART CENTER

Creative Growth Art Center, a nonprofit art studio and gallery for artists with disabilities, was founded in 1974 by Florence Ludins-Katz and Elias Katz. They developed a program that provides working space, supplies, and nondirective support to participating artists. In the 1980s, the Katzes bought the former automobile paint and body shop, which was part of Auto Row. The building was built in 1926 and is now divided among studio space, a gallery, dining areas, and offices. The public art gallery hosts regular exhibitions of Creative Growth's artists and offers them representation in the contemporary art world.

ABOVE The large windows of the former auto body repair shop are practical for an art studio and gallery.

BELOW A skylight brings natural light into the gallery, which is connected to the studio via a ramp.

ABOVE Artists work at tables in the shared studio space.

BELOW The dining room mural was a collaboration by artists in the studio in 2014.

MEI-LAN TAN AND VICTOR LEFEBVRE STUDIO AND RESIDENCE

Neither Mei-Lan Tan nor Victor Lefebvre is from Oakland (she's from Los Angeles and he's from France), but they've made the city their home and the center of their growing design business, UMÉ Studio, since 2016. They live in West Oakland, in the industrial McClymonds neighborhood, in a 6,000-square-foot, two-level space that was built inside the 1924 California Towel Company factory. Upstairs is used for living and downstairs is the company's production studio and showroom.

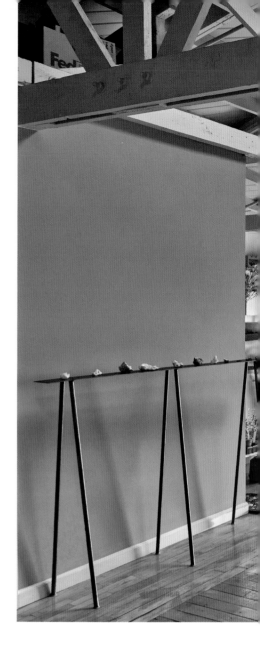

LEFT, TOP Their bright office area is below the second-floor residential section.

LEFT, BOTTOM The courtyard entry of the studio has a container garden and sliding metal door.

ABOVE The designers have prototypes of their own furniture in the upstairs living area. Their steel Paper Table is placed against a wall. "It is essential for us to be surrounded not only by the objects we make but by our friends' creations, things we love, things from our travels," says Lefebvre. "We come from different parts in the world with very different backgrounds and we like to see our space as a mix of all of this."

OPPOSITE The designers Mei-Lan Tan and Victor Lefebvre have worked together in this loft since 2016.

In the production studio, Tan and Lefebvre kept the original wooden trusses of the ceiling, double-height windows, and exposed brick wall. The designers make, show, and ship their work from here.

RONALD RAEL AND VIRGINIA SAN FRATELLO'S BACKYARD CABIN

Ronald Rael and Virginia San Fratello are architects, artists, and educators. Their passion is 3-D-printed architecture. Through their design studio/thinktank, Emerging Objects, they've been experimenting with the process of upcycling used cement, sawdust, clay, and even grape skins as material for building. In 2016, when the city of Oakland voted to ease restrictions on backyard buildings, Rael and San Fratello decided to make a cabin in their own backyard from tiles produced by 3-D printers in a process called paste extrusion.

ABOVE The cabin took about 18 months from start to finish for the couple to build, with some help.

BELOW Hexagonal-shaped tiles with room for succulent plants make up the front of the cabin, which is weatherproof.

OPPOSITE The interiors are made of an opaque bio-plastic that reveals its translucence when lit from behind. The architects loved the way the colors change the mood and atmosphere of the cabin.

TASSAFARONGA
VILLAGE'S
PASTA FACTORY

David Baker Architects is well-known for designing affordable housing projects using older buildings. One of their projects incorporated an empty pasta factory into a new neighborhood named Tassafaronga Village, which is located in South Oakland. The old factory was converted into small apartments.

ABOVE Private balconies in steel were added to the former pasta factory.

BELOW The architects created a new entryway.

OPPOSITE, ABOVE Solar-power panels were included in the design to provide electricity and water heating, which in turn helped to achieve the LEED standards for green design.

OPPOSITE, BELOW The original signage of the pasta factory was repainted on the outside of the new apartment building.

TEMESCAL
ALLEYS

The Temescal Alleys are two pedestrian-friendly shopping streets located in one of Oakland's oldest neighborhoods. The small artisanal shops that line the alleys are installed in what once were horse stalls off one of the main streets, Telegraph Avenue. Most of the vendors are local California companies.

The shops have adapted their designs to fit their individual brands, which is part of their charm. The bookstore, for example, uses barn-door hinges for its main entrance, while the café has folding glass doors.

ABOVE   Low rise buildings with tiled roof details are at entrance of one of the shopping streets.

BELOW   There's café seating at the front entrance of one alley near the floral shop.

PORT

**THE TELEVISION SHOW *PORTLANDIA*
BROUGHT** Portland national attention.
The city's style has been described as
"crunchy" and "hipster." However, its
natural splendor defines the place. From
April to fall, rhododendron bushes in
bright shades of white, pink, purple, and
red—in some cases larger than the houses
they are planted in front of—bloom in and
around Portland's neighborhoods. Fragrant
climbing roses cover the trellises and
fences. Native Douglas fir trees grow on
the hillsides. The natural environment is
is striking, beautiful, and memorable, and
seemingly at odds with the city's industrial
past. Portland has 12 bridges that cross
over the Willamette River, connecting the
east and west sides of town. The river has
brought commerce and commodities since
the city's founding. Logging, trading, and
transportation changed a wooded place to a
center of business. The contrast between the
two and the ability to merge them together
has people flocking to the Pacific Northwest

city. As it has become a more desirable
place to live, the cost of housing has
increased, and people feel priced out of
their neighborhoods. Yet Portlanders pride
themselves on an open, welcoming attitude
to newcomers. One reflection of this spirit
of inclusivity is the communal gatherings
around the food truck scene—you never
know who you might meet standing in line
for a taco. Food trucks are the city's
experiential kitchens, which congregate in
parking-lot spots not only in the inner city
but also in the suburbs. Each one focuses
on a different cuisine or specialty, from
pad thai, to fried chicken, to tacos, and
beyond. Warehouses in the Pearl District
dating from the late 1800s have been
redeveloped as retail and shopping venues.
One of the area's most famous destinations
is the sprawling Powell's bookstore, which
in its room-to-room, section-by-section,
floor-to-ceiling organization models the
city's neighborhoods and character—varied,
changing, and color filled.

PORTLAND
JAPANESE
GARDEN

The Portland Japanese Garden opened in 1961 on the site of the old zoo in Washington Park, in northwest Portland. The garden was designed by Professor Takuma Tono of Tokyo Agricultural University as a "healing gesture" between the American and Japanese cultures after World War ll. In 2017, architect Kengo Kuma was commissioned to design the Cultural Village expansion. It was his first public project in the United States. The village consists of three buildings surrounding a wide courtyard. With their tiered roofs—the upper one covered in plantings—the Learning Center and garden house disappear into the landscape, especially when viewed from below, on the paths of the Strolling Pond Garden.

RIGHT The Umami Café, positioned near the entrance staircase, floats above the garden landscape.

OPPOSITE, ABOVE The new Learning Center can be seen from the lower garden path.

OPPOSITE, BELOW The Cultural Village was added to the Portland Japanese Garden in 2017.

JEAN VOLLUM NATURAL CAPITAL CENTER

Ecotrust, an environmental nonprofit organization, was looking for a permanent home base. In 1998, they purchased the 70,000-square-foot J. McCracken warehouse, as well as the building next door, in Portland's River District. With a team of architects, designers, and sustainability experts, they set out to transform the old warehouse into not only their own headquarters but also a place where similar-minded eco-friendly companies could rent space, with the intent of creating a community. The result of a nearly four-year process is the Jean Vollum Natural Capital Center. The thoughtful alterations by Holst Architecture and sustainability consultant Gregory Acker Architect included adding a third floor with a roof deck and a fireplace, installing steel towers on the exterior for structural support, and incorporating skylights, which provide natural light to the second-floor office spaces. As the natural plantings are encouraged to grow on the building's exterior, it appears there is a total synthesis of architecture and an environmental mission.

OPPOSITE, TOP Inside, the original post-and-beam construction was the basis for the renovation. The Douglas fir floor planks and brickwork of the old warehouse were also preserved, while bridges of glass and steel connect the new office spaces.

OPPOSITE, BOTTOM LEFT Steel staircases on the back of the building were built for additional structural support but also to allow access to the new third-floor addition.

OPPOSITE, BOTTOM RIGHT The remaining brick structures of the building next door frame both the lot and the natural surroundings.

ABOVE The plant-covered back entrance of the Ecotrust building shows through to its parking lot next door. The organization developed the historic warehouse as well as the site next door, which includes parking for bicycles and contains remnants of the old building.

SWIFT

Swift—known for its cutting-edge creative campaigns for clients such as Adidas, Fitbit, Twitter, and other lifestyle brands—has an equally cutting-edge headquarters in the Slabtown neighborhood of Northwest Portland. The former Rose City Awning building, with its sawtooth roof windows, was designed to suit the agency's collaborative process, which included adding more and different types of meeting areas, such as hallways with standing desks, tables with benches, and a sunken conversation pit. The glass front entry of the office that architecture firm Beebe Skidmore created draws visitors into the light-filled atrium that serves as a nexus of the activities of the company. Just off the entrance, a space for impromptu meetings includes tables with bench seating.

ABOVE The agency's manifesto is painted on an exterior corner in black and white paint.

BELOW The rear entrance of Swift shows the new sawtooth design that was added to the existing structure by architects Beebe Skidmore and picks up on the original building's roofline.

The wood beams of the original factory not only provide support for the skylights to the interior atrium but also an element of natural warmth.

The conversation pit, just off the atrium hallway, is surrounded by interior plants. The angle of the sawtooth rooftop becomes a motif that is reflected throughout the interior decoration. Architecture firm Beebe Skidmore was also responsible for the interior design.

HI-LO HOTEL

The Hi-Lo Hotel in Portland's downtown was once known as the Oregon Pioneer Building. The former office building, built in 1910, was added to the US National Register of Historic Places in 1979. It is notable for its reinforced concrete structure—one of the first in Portland. The hotel became part of Marriott's Autograph Collection after a renovation by Portland-based Jessica Helgerson Interior Design in 2018. The interior design program was to combine elements of high-end luxury, such as the elegant fabrics and low-slung-style furniture of the front lobbies and bar, with rudimentary structural materials like the concrete pillars and walls of the original construction.

ABOVE The Hi-Lo Hotel sits on a corner in downtown Portland. Arched windows are a feature of the low-rise, six-floor edifice.

BELOW Upstairs in the guest rooms, the dark wood creates a nook for a sofa and complements the raw concrete pillars that are a running theme throughout the hotel design.

ABOVE The lobby of the hotel has low-slung green velvet seating which offers an intimate space for conversations. Floor-to-ceiling windows flood the lobby with light.

BELOW The restaurant on the ground floor, CRAFTpdx, also has the exposed concrete walls with leather banquettes in rust and grey.

The soft gray of the concrete wall offered color-palette inspiration for one of the three seating areas in the ground-floor lobby. Pink chairs and a suspended loveseat complete the look.

THE ZIPPER

To call the Zipper a food court is completely inaccurate, although it technically is a gathering of restaurants around two seating areas, one inside and one out. The brainchild of developer Kevin Cavenaugh's company Guerrilla Development, the Zipper is so much cooler than that—it's a lesson in community planning all in one block. The former used-car lot was transformed into a hub for four micro-restaurants, a nail salon, and a coffee shop in 2015. As for the cool factor, first, there is the lenticular-like artwork by Yoskay Yamamoto, Gage Hamilton, and the artist duo known as Cyrcle, David Leavitt and David Torres, on the outside of the long facade that runs from the corner of NE Sandy Boulevard and NE 27th Avenue. Then there is the punk rock nail salon. And finally, there is the backyard and community dining areas, whose vibe is casual and relaxed, which leads to interesting conversations and connections.

The artwork on the exterior of the Zipper can be viewed from two different angles, coming and going on both NE Sandy Boulevard and NE 27th Avenue.

ABOVE After patrons order their food from one of the four restaurants inside the Zipper, they can sit at the shared community picnic tables on the outdoor terrace.

BELOW The unique artwork disappears in a side view of the Zipper's exterior. Wooden slats hide and revel the paintings.

CINCINNATI HAS HAD ITS SHARE of highs and lows since its founding in 1788—from being a Midwest powerhouse of industry considered the Queen of the West (hence its nickname, the Queen City), to racial tensions that culminated in a riot in downtown in 2001, to once again being a center of big business. Corporations such as Proctor & Gamble and Kroger have corporate headquarters there and General Electric has built an operations hub in the riverfront development named the Banks. A lot of the attention surrounding Cincinnati's revitalization has been focused on the neighborhood known as Over-the-Rhine (OTR). The moniker refers to perhaps one of the largest intact historic districts in the country, according to the Over-the-Rhine Foundation. At one time, the Miami and Erie Canal divided the area from the Central Business District, and it was referred to as the Rhine by the German immigrants who worked and lived nearby. In the 19th and mid-20th centuries, OTR was also home to a large concentration of breweries. Recently, beermaking has returned, along with new restaurants, coffee shops, and other retail, creating a lively scene. In addition to the historical housing stock, Findlay Market, opened in 1852, continues to draw locals and visitors to its food vendors. On Washington Park, the Cincinnati Music Hall completed a full restoration in 2017. Yet OTR isn't the only place where there is evidence of reinvestment. The reuse of old buildings is spreading out of the city center to neighborhoods such as Oakley and across the river to Covington, Kentucky.

21c MUSEUM HOTEL

Cofounders of 21c Museum Hotels Laura Lee Brown and Steve Wilson developed the concept of integrating art into the world of hospitality design, combining their interests in art, preservation, and community. The 21c Museum Hotel in Cincinnati is a great example of their idea in practice. The original Metropole Hotel was built in 1912 and the building later became low-income housing, falling into disrepair in the 1970s. Architects Deborah Berke Partners were brought in to create new spaces to display artworks, 156 guest rooms, a spa, and a rooftop lounge as well as to preserve historic features of the old hotel. Art is on display throughout, from vitrines on each floor that are filled with local artists' work to tiny sculptures designed by the architects and installed in the showers. The ground-floor gallery is open to the public and presents changing exhibits. Even the restaurant, Metropole, is used as exhibition space.

OPPOSITE, ABOVE The Metropole Hotel was built in 1912. 21c Museum Hotels completed the $50 million renovation of the building in 2012.

OPPOSITE, BELOW An artwork by Ryan Wolfe titled *Field of Grass* is on display in the stairwell to the rooftop spa.

ABOVE An artwork, *Yellow Penguin* by Cracking Art Group, is placed on a cornice above the dining room of Metropole restaurant.

A lightwell became an exhibition space for Astrid Krogh's hanging artwork *Lightmail*.

LOIS AND RICHARD ROSENTHAL CENTER FOR CONTEMPORARY ART

The Lois and Richard Rosenthal Center for Contemporary Art was architect Zaha Hadid's first project in the United States as well as the first museum designed by a woman architect in the United States. The new structure, completed in 2003, is sited on a busy intersection across from the Aronoff Center for the Arts, and next door to the 21c Museum Hotel, creating a cultural corner downtown. Hadid's double concept for the building was first an "urban carpet" that welcomes pedestrians from the sidewalk inside and upstairs, and second, a "jigsaw puzzle" that refers to the varied scale of the upper galleries. In 2015, the lobby was renovated by architects FRCH to include a restaurant, bar, and movable gift shop.

ABOVE The exterior of the Lois and Richard Rosenthal Center for Contemporary Art shows the glass frontage of the lobby entrance and the massing of concrete galleries above.

BELOW Hadid designed a series of intersecting ramps and stairways between the floors of galleries.

Hadid's "urban carpet" concept extends through the lobby in the form of a concrete ramp. A light installation by Erwin Redl is mounted on the wall. The kite-like work, *Solar Belle* by Tomás Saraceno floats above.

URBANA CAFÉ

Daniel Noguera started his coffee business by converting a Vespa l'Ape utility motorcycle into a mobile espresso bar. He parked at Findlay Market and from there created a company that now has a second mobile unit and two brick-and-mortar locations.

ABOVE Daniel Noguera and his converted l'Ape espresso bar.

BELOW Urbana Café's first shop is in the Pendleton neighborhood near Findlay Market. The interiors were stripped down to the brick exterior walls in keeping with spirit of the 19th-century district. In addition to coffee, Noguera serves house-made pastries.

FINDLAY MARKET

Findlay Market has been a food destination since it opened in the Over-the-Rhine neighborhood in the mid-1800s. The market is a testing ground for new food businesses, but it is also a permanent home to year-round companies such as butchers, a cheese monger, and chocolatiers. Seasonal stalls surround the exterior, especially in the summer, when pop-up stands are popular. The market is an active part of the surrounding community and town. The Findlay Market Opening Day Parade for the Cincinnati Reds is famous citywide.

ABOVE Inside the main market shed there are more than 50 permanent food vendors, along with seating for customers.

BELOW Outside the market building there are additional stalls and more food-related establishments and restaurants. The alleyways are filled with café tables and chairs in warmer weather.

A mural by artist D*Face, titled *Tainted Love//My Mistakes Were Made for You*, was installed on the building as part of the BLINK light and art festival.

HUGHES RESIDENCE AT ARTICHOKE CURATED COOKWARE COLLECTION

Bradley and Karen Hughes live over their shop, Artichoke Curated Cookware Collection, which sells high-end kitchen products and is a block from Findlay Market. They bought the three-story building in April 2015 and moved in just about a year later. Since OTR is a historic district and this property was built around 1885, their architect, Terry Boling, took special care in the renovation, working within a series of rules and guidelines. However, the building's program didn't change—the first floor was always retail and the upper floors were always residential. What did change were the modern interiors and, on the exterior, balconies were added, as was a black perforated-steel staircase tower.

ABOVE AND BELOW The new design of the floor-through loft residence includes two cherry wood "cubes" that contain storage space in the bedrooms and at the entry.

NEIL MARQUARDT AND LAUREN KLAR RESIDENCE

Neil Marquardt and Lauren Klar first entered this 19th-century warehouse in the Over-the-Rhine district as party crashers—they were looking to buy a building next door but the sounds from a rave with 400 guests drew them inside. Less than six months later, they purchased the property and took on a very personal project—a new home with a walled garden. The couple, who were the main designers, worked with architect Mike Wentz to make decisions, such as to keep the existing original brick facade, which dates to the late 1890s, and to construct a new two-story house that takes up about one-third of the lot. The remaining portion is a walled-in outdoor area. Evidence of the building's previous life, such as beams from the former warehouse, are part of the backyard's new design, which now includes a swimming pool, bar, and patio. Stepping on the rear deck feels like a time-travel adventure, with one foot in the 21st century while looking at the remnants of another.

OPPOSITE, ABOVE A glass and steel staircase connects the entry level to the second floor, while a glass bridge connects the master suite with the guest area.

OPPOSITE, BELOW In sharp contrast to the facade and back garden, the interiors, including the new kitchen, are sleek and modern.

ABOVE Through the sliding glass doors of the living room, one can see the remaining brick walls of the old warehouse that surround the new garden, affectionately named "Broccoli's Run" after the owners' dog.

BELOW A view of the house from the backyard shows the swimming pool, deck, and bar, but also how the modern house fits in the footprint of the old building.

MADTREE BREWING COMPANY

MadTree Brewing Company is located in Oakley, an east side neighborhood of Cincinnati named for the sharp-shooter Annie Oakley. The business was started by Brady Duncan, Kenny McNutt, and Jeff Hunt, who took over an old paper-making plant in 2017 and turned it into a taproom, beer garden, and brewery. All the elements of beermaking production, including packaging and the quality lab, are located just off the taproom, where behind a wood-framed counter, Catch-A-Fire makes wood-fired pizzas. Outside, the remaining brick facade and its steel beams create the patio of the beer garden.

ABOVE MadTree Brewing's beer garden with its outdoor fire pit was created by leaving the remnants of the old brick paper plant.

BELOW The stainless grist case above the pilot brew-house holds crushed grain used to make craft beer.

ABOVE The main floor of the taproom is 25,000 square feet. The beermaking process is on full display, with tanks behind the picnic tables for customers.

BELOW One of the two bars in the taproom serves 40 or more beers. Some of the building's original moldings and windows, which were meant to represent a German rathskeller, were integrated into the contemporary design.

RHINEGEIST BREWERY

Up a couple of metal staircases that are totally covered in stickers of all sorts, from everywhere, is a huge open space—it feels like the size of a football field. Big Ass fans circulate wafts of brewing hops. Gigantic stainless-steel tanks are all within view of the patrons who stop in to try the more than 40 beers on offer. There are two bars, and picnic tables are placed throughout, as are cornhole games. This is home of Rhinegeist Brewery, started in 2013 by Bob Bonder and Bryant Goulding, who then brought in master brewer Jim Matt. The brewery is actually three buildings linked together—one is the former site of early Cincinnati brewer Christian Moerlein's original bottling facility, dating back to 1896; the second is a 1912 bottling facility; and the last is a structure built in 1924 by Arthur Nash Tailoring Company. By reclaiming these old spaces, Rhinegeist Brewery brings the Over-the-Rhine neighborhood's fascinating history of beermaking full circle.

HOTEL
COVINGTON

Just across the Ohio River from Cincinnati in Covington, Kentucky, the 1909 Coppin's Department Store was converted into the 114-room Hotel Covington. The $22 million renovation by the owners, Aparium Hotel Group and the Salyers Group, completed in 2016, included incorporating the facade of the storefront next door into the property, and transforming its footprint into an open-air patio. The new renovation was led by Hub + Weber Architects and Plume Interiors + Light. The architects and designers left details such as the eight seven-sided columns that ran down the first-floor shopping concourse and took advantage of the floor-to-ceiling windows to create a brightened lobby with a bar and multiple sitting areas.

LEFT A painting by Donna Talerico and advertisements from Coppin's Department Store are displayed in the lobby of the Hotel Covington.

ABOVE The restaurant Coppin's extends into the courtyard created between the hotel and the building next door.

OPPOSITE, LEFT An intricate iron gate by Stewart Iron Works was placed behind the check-in desk. A small gift shop features local merchandise displayed in the front window of the hotel.

OPPOSITE, RIGHT The lobby—with its plush velvet chairs and sofas—was designed for lingering. Custom glass chandeliers by Stillpass Studio are installed above the seating. Brass shelving divides the front-desk check-in from the large open-plan room.

MOND

"IN RICHMOND, THE RIVER IS EVERYTHING," declares Isaac Regelson—an architect and location scout who grew up playing and exploring along the James River. Richmond, Virginia, was founded in 1737, although settlers had been on the riverbanks since around 1607 and Native Americans before that. Transportation and trade took place along the water, and industries such as tobacco, mining, and banking developed there as well. A diverse economy prevented the lows that other cities experience when a major industry leaves. However, in modern times, the center city suffered as people moved away from downtown and I-95 cut a swath through some neighborhoods. While its Confederate past is not forgotten (landmarks and monuments to its generals stand along leafy boulevards), an alternative history, one that is inclusive and offers a more complex story, is emerging and is on view—at the Black History Museum, for example. A new neighborhood, Scott's Addition, has developed out of an industrial warehouse district. Today, the river is a center for recreation and regrowth as well. Running trails, beaches, lofts, and apartment houses line the waterway. Contemporary architecture and art, craft breweries and restaurants, and an infusion of fresh entrepreneurs are telling a different story of Richmond, one that embraces the energy of the river—quietly relentless.

BLACK HISTORY MUSEUM AND CULTURAL CENTER OF VIRGINIA

Located in the historic Jackson Ward district, the former Leigh Street Armory for the African American Militia of Virginia was converted into a museum that exhibits artifacts, photographic material, and objects celebrating African Americans in Virginia. The museum moved into the space after a two-year restoration, which included the addition of a glass, steel, and brick public entrance on the ground level and additional space upstairs, all designed by the Baskervill firm, based in Richmond.

ABOVE The front facade has a symmetrical design with two brick turrets on each corner. Both are visible from Abner Clay Park across the street.

BELOW The new addition used materials such as brick, glass, and steel to honor the older building in front.

AMERICAN CIVIL WAR MUSEUM AT HISTORIC TREDEGAR

ABOVE A view of the campus from Brown's Island includes a glimpse of the original Gun Foundry and two new buildings, the entry pavilion and the museum designed by local firm 3north.

BELOW The Gun Foundry Building with its brick facade and courtyard is one of the few remaining historical buildings that is central to the museum grounds.

The American Civil War Museum has two sites in Richmond, the White House of the Confederacy and Historic Tredegar. Historic Tredegar is located on the grounds of the Tredegar Iron Works, which opened in 1836 and was in use until the late 1950s. During the Civil War, the foundry produced munitions for the Confederacy. In 2006, several remaining structures were transformed into a campus that includes exhibition halls and education rooms. The museum holds more than 15,000 objects in its collection. Some 500 of these artifacts are on display, helping to tell the story of the war from three perspectives, Union, Confederate, and African American. The process of renovation and expansion is ongoing—a new building was finished in 2019.

ABOVE A view of the stairwell captures the openness between floors.

RIGHT The Forum is on the entry level.

OPPOSITE The intersection—even at night—is always active. The ICA galleries harness that energy and welcome in the community.

THE MARKEL CENTER AT VIRGINIA COMMONWEALTH UNIVERSITY

Designed by Steven Holl Architects, the Markel Center opened in the spring of 2018 and houses the Institute for Contemporary Art (ICA) at Virginia Commonwealth University. The building is sited on one of Richmond's busy downtown intersections and marks a place where the city meets the campus. It contains four exhibition galleries, a 240-seat performance space, a café, and an outdoor sculpture garden. The street-level entry, with its soaring ceiling and wall of windows, is named the Forum. It fosters connections as visitors easily move between galleries or wait in the space for performances to begin in the theater. The second entrance is through the garden, by the reflecting pool, and between the galleries that are projected above. The building's materials—pre-weathered titanium zinc and matte translucent glass—seem incongruous with the brick buildings nearby, but at night, with its interior lights ablaze, the Markel Center appears as a beacon, holding true to the ICA's mission of exhibiting the "art of our time."

QUIRK HOTEL

Richmonders Ted and Katie Ukrop decided to open a small 75-room hotel in the area known as the Arts District. Their project transformed the 1916 building that was once home to the J. B. Mosby and Company department store and a smaller building next door. The two structures contain the main hotel and a gallery/gift shop, with a courtyard in the space in between. On the ground floor, the renovation included making a lobby and restaurant while keeping the dramatic black-iron stair-case, the groin-vault ceiling, and segmental arches and columns. Upstairs, the interior designers, Robert Bristow and Pilar Proffitt, kept the room furnishings minimal, with a few select pieces, yet warm, with details such as beds made from reclaimed wood and a pink color palette. The hotel has become a meeting spot for not only visitors or tourists but also locals who are taking in the gallery scene and want to admire the city from the rooftop bar.

ABOVE The six-story Quirk Hotel, a former department store in the Richmond Arts District, has arched windows on its facade and along the side of the building.

BELOW A gold reception desk greets guests. Shelving behind the counter displays artifacts from the former department store.

ABOVE The restaurant in the hotel lobby is named Maple & Pine.

BELOW The front corner windows of the lobby illuminate a cozy seating area. The color pink is found throughout the hotel, in upholstery, wall colors, and accessories.

MOBELUX

Jeff Rock and Garrett Ross, the founders of Mobelux, a digital design agency, went through the process of turning an 80-year-old post office—the Saunders Station—into their modern office space. The first step was buying the building from the US Department of the Interior. Next, they set out to restore the station and leave in place as many of the existing elements of the old post office as possible. These details included the marble wainscoting and the original post office boxes. However, the team, along with the architect, Bob Steele, changed and adapted various aspects of the old interiors. They moved the steel doors that were once in the front lobby and reused them as sliding doors in the agency's open-plan office. The postmaster's office was turned into a small conference room and the main counter was restored to its original place. A photograph of a mural by Works Progress Administration (WPA) artist Julien Binford, printed on stretched canvas, once proposed for the first station, is finally exhibited in the lobby. Its subject matter—the burning of Richmond—was too controversial to be displayed in the 1930s. Downstairs, Rock and Ross added a high-tech theater, a billiards room, and lounge, modern amenities that are now part of innovative workspaces.

TOP Looking through the main workplace, which was the former sorting floor of the old post office, to the new employee cafeteria extension.

MIDDLE The Mobelux office—the former Saunders Station post office—is located in the Fan District.

BOTTOM Old post office boxes on three walls were restored and have become part of the interior design.

The front lobby features a facsimile
of a black-and-white painting by
WPA artist Julien Binford.

The window-service lobby was transformed into a waiting room for the agency.

ABOVE A view from the corner of the renovated tenement and the new extension shows the old and new sections combined.

BELOW One side of the tenement residence is now the dining room and has a staircase and fireplace.

OPPOSITE, ABOVE The connection between the old building and the new one is represented by two windows—one modern, one historic.

OPPOSITE, BELOW Downstairs, the family room has a wall of windows all around.

TODD AND NEELY DYKSHORN RESIDENCE

Todd Dykshorn, an architect, was so attentive to the renovation of his family's 19th-century duplex tenement in the Church Hill neighborhood of Richmond that he and his wife, Neely, an editor, moved next door during the construction. While adding on to an old building takes special care, the Dykshorns were also restoring the existing features of the old structure. There are few examples of this type of pre–Civil War housing in the area. "The goal was to redefine the original house," says Todd. An earlier extension that added a kitchen and bathrooms had fallen into disrepair and was removed. The new modern steel-and-glass addition extended the kitchen and contained a sitting room downstairs and a master bedroom upstairs. But you would never know it from the street, unless you looked at the now-unified house from the corner, where you can catch sight of the new structure peeking out from the backyard. Historic Richmond, a non-profit preservation organization, rewarded their efforts in 2018.

BLUE BEE CIDER

Courtney Mailey left the corporate world and immersed herself in the cider business. She founded Blue Bee Cider, named after the blue orchard bee, an important part of the apple tree pollination process. When Blue Bee was looking for a new home, she purchased the Summit Stables, former municipal stables in the Scott's Addition neighborhood. The complex of cobblestone buildings is organized around a courtyard that is now used for community events, cornhole games, and tastings.

ABOVE The cobblestone buildings were restored and repurposed to produce the Blue Bee ciders, which meant incorporating all the elements of cider production, including stainless steel tanks and wood barrels, into the old stable. The original doors were kept and add authenticity to the cidery courtyard.

OPPOSITE, RIGHT The building standing perpendicular to the street houses the tasting room and looks into the courtyard. All the buildings were made from recycled cobblestones from the city of Richmond.

OPPOSITE, FAR RIGHT Above the courtyard, an event room with yellow heart pine floors is used for private parties. It was used as the hayloft for the mules' feed.

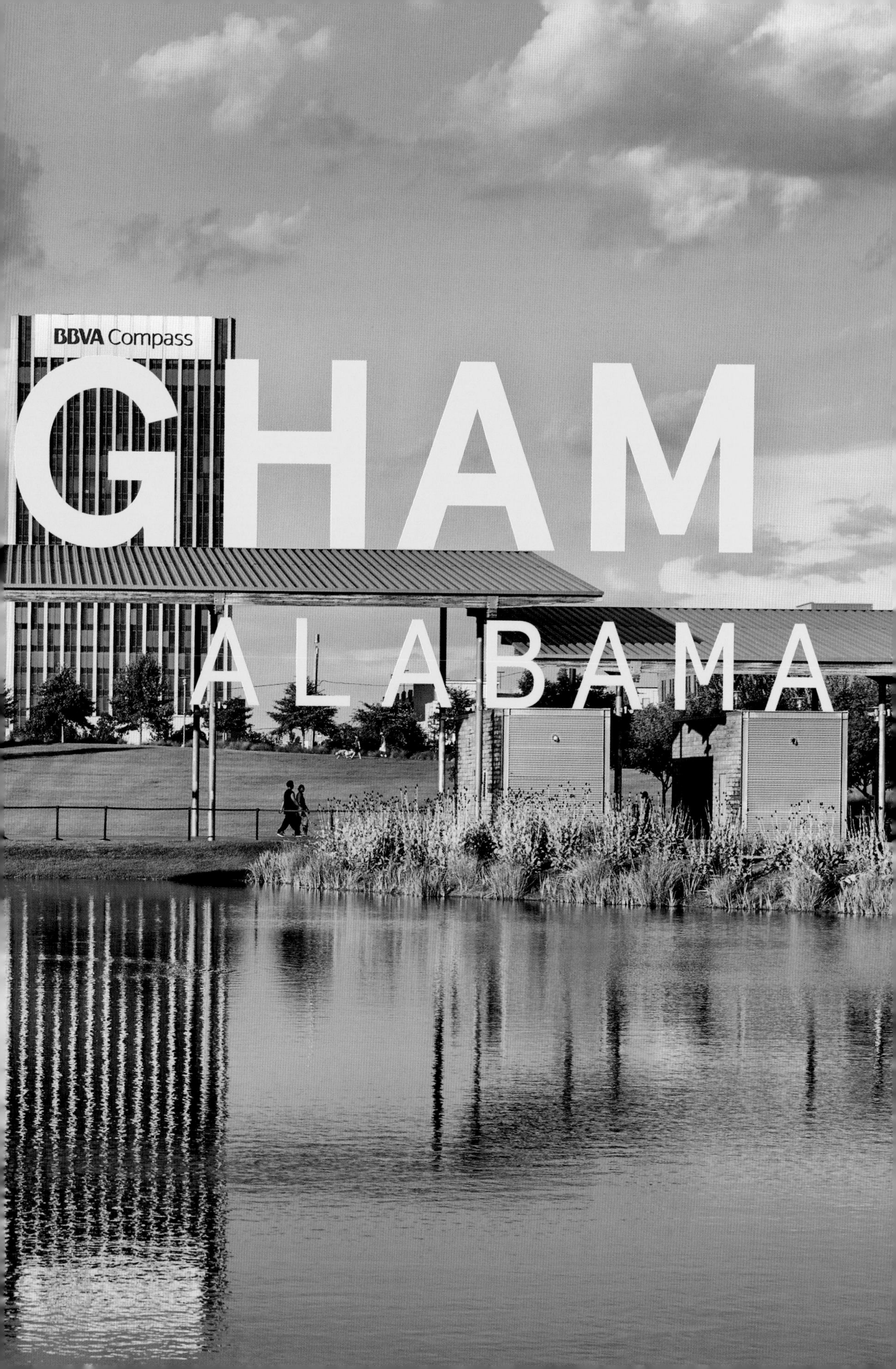
BBVA Compass
GHAM
ALABAMA

THE CITY OF BIRMINGHAM, ALABAMA, sits in the Jones Valley of Red Mountain and was founded in 1871 at the crossing of two railroads. Almost 150 years later, the railroad still plays an important part in Birmingham's civic life. In 2010, Railroad Park, a 19-acre urban park, opened in downtown. The beautifully designed park with its walking paths, shelters, and lake offers a respite to everyone who lives, visits, or works nearby. Railroad Park is connected to other parts of town via the Rotary Trail—which benefited from the federal government's Rails-to-Trails program—promoting a walkable city that recalls its glory days, when iron ore was the industry that brought prosperity. At one time, US Steel was one of the largest employers and Birmingham was known as the "Pittsburgh of the South." The Sloss Furnaces that once produced the pig iron used in the artillery of World War II are now a museum and an entertainment venue.

A 56-foot-tall iron statue of Vulcan, the Roman god of fire and forge, overlooks the city from a wooded ridge and pays homage to this industrial legacy. At the same time, Birmingham's important place in the nation's civil rights history is recognized at the Birmingham Civil Rights Institute and at the 16th Street Baptist Church. With its history honored and on display, Birmingham doesn't feel stuck in its complicated past. Stop for a moment at the farmers' market at Pepper Place and the budding diversity of the town reveals itself—young families and older adults of all races mingle among the peach and tomato stands. The University of Alabama at Birmingham, known as one of the leading medical research facilities, is now one of the town's largest employers. Maker centers such as Innovation Depot and MAKEbhm are developing a new generation of entrepreneurs that are helping to make Birmingham a crossroads of creativity.

PEPPER PLACE

The former Dr. Pepper Bottling Company buildings are now the site of a garden shop, a farmers' and makers' market, and multiple restaurants and businesses. There is over 350,000 square feet in the old manufacturing and bottling facility that was once part of the soft drink's network, which originated in Texas in the 1920s. The 1988 development of these reclaimed properties was one of the first adaptive reuse projects in Birmingham and helped to establish the Lakeview Design District— a thriving nexus of the community.

TOP The brick bottling plant of the soft drink Dr. Pepper opened in the 1920s and reopened almost 70 years later as a mixed-use development.

MIDDLE AND OPPOSITE A walk through the verdant Pepper Place goes through Charlie Thigpen's Garden Gallery. The shop's wares, including plants and sculptures, spill outside and over the building.

BOTTOM The Market at Pepper Place on a busy Saturday morning includes all types of vendors and people, from bakers and farmers to students and young families.

BRÄT BROT GARTENBAR

The owner of Brät Brot, David Carrigan, gave architect Bruce Lanier the program: transform a former plant nursery into a German biergarten. Lanier took a cheeky approach to the design of the casual restaurant that serves house-made German sausages and specialty beers. Through the stone facade front entrance, a taxidermy wild boar sets the scene in a large glass vitrine display case. Just inside the greenhouse, under a glass roof, is the main barroom with a circular bar, communal tables, and pebble gravel floors. In the back, there are gardens outside under shady trees, where patrons enjoy food and outdoor games.

ABOVE A display of taxidermy by artist Bunny Lane is installed at the entrance. The wild boar has become a motif for the restaurant.

Community tables—a modern version of the picnic table in wood and steel—create the dining area inside.

ABOVE The unique gabled entry of the original building—a plant nursery—became a feature in the new design.

BELOW The carved circular limestone bar is the center of the room and a gathering place to collect the beers on tap.

SLOSS FURNACES

The Sloss Furnaces opened in 1881 and over 100 years later, in 1983, became a museum. The transformation of the site and its structures from the workhorse and backbone of the Birmingham economy to an entertainment district is a reflection of the city's trajectory. The City Furnaces, as they were known, produced pig iron from their opening until the early 1970s. There are two blast furnaces on site that date from the turn of the century, plus 40 outbuildings. Today, the furnaces are used not only as a museum and backdrops for cultural events such as music and beer festivals, and for community activities such as conferences and meetings, but also for a metal-arts education program.

TOP The exterior of the furnaces has corroded over time, producing a deep red color. Part of the stabilization of the site included adding protective coatings to slow further corrosion.

MIDDLE The Sloss Furnaces have been preserved and were given National Historic Landmark status in 1981.

BOTTOM The newly built visitor and education center designed by architect Fred Keith opened in 2012.

BACK FORTY BEER COMPANY

Doug Brown opened the microbrewery Back Forty Beer Company in July 2018. He was looking for a place that allowed the company to pursue its mission: offering an ever-changing selection of 30 to 40 different beers made onsite. The building he chose was a warehouse for the Sloss Furnaces, located across the street. At one time, railroad tracks ran directly into what is now the taproom. The industrial space offered the large footprint needed for beermaking, cooking, and dining areas. When renovating, Brown and his crew kept the concrete walls and steel-beam rafters and made an outdoor garden in the front.

TOP The brewhouse, with its fermentation vessels and brite tanks, is located in the warehouse. A local artisan, Greg Steffens, hand carved the tap handles from wood remnants.

MIDDLE Inside food and beer is served at long tables. Ductwork, beams, and concrete are part of the décor.

BOTTOM The exterior of the brewery features an outdoor beer garden and lawn, where kids can play. Families are the brewery's best customers.

INNOVATION DEPOT

An empty Sears, Roebuck department store in downtown Birmingham was gutted and converted into an entrepreneur center and wet labs for the University of Alabama at Birmingham. The project was a collaboration between the City of Birmingham and UAB. In order to accommodate a range of programs for young companies in their startup phase to those that cater to established businesses the space was planned in the most flexible way possible. There are large meeting rooms for courses, smaller private offices, and community areas that foster collaborations among the Depot's members and visitors. While walking through the long corridors, one can only imagine the floors of the old department store—in fact, many in the community used to shop at the former store. But the conversion has created a more modern and industrial-looking space that took the interiors back to their structural materials—concrete and steel.

ABOVE Hallway seating areas, inserted into the floor-to-ceiling window bays, double as meeting rooms.

BELOW A steel staircase and elevator to the second floor was added to the former department store.

MAKEbhm

When architect Bruce Lanier was looking for a home for his own woodworking shop, he recognized a need for a maker's hub and coworking space. He looked for a building that could accommodate studios for artists and artisans and workspaces for small companies and professionals. He found a 22,000-square-foot warehouse in the Birmingham neighborhood Avondale. When planning the space, he studied and experimented with different types of facilities that would be useful and draw tenants, and as a result the space has a woodshop and a ceramic kiln available for communal use by the residents. Lanier also considered how the project would fit into the neighborhood, which has become a food destination with a plethora of restaurants. He made the decision to bring an ice cream shop, Big Spoon Creamery, to the front retail space.

TOP The truck for Big Spoon Creamery is often parked in the entry of MAKEbhm.

MIDDLE The courtyard for MAKEbhm has a patio for the ice cream shop, Big Spoon Creamery, that is also used by the resident makers and tenants.

BOTTOM A view from above shows the Susan Gordon Pottery and the wood shop of Alabama Sawyer, a wood furniture and products company.

CHERYL MORGAN RESIDENCE

Cheryl Morgan, an architect and emirita professor and director of Auburn University Urban Studio program, renovated a 1910 warehouse that had quite a past, mainly as a site for manufacturing—everything from flour to aluminum doors and windows. The front of the building has two stories and the living space has a mezzanine. Morgan kept many of the existing elements, including the heart pine floors, the steel beams, and the wooden columns. However, the most defining element of the home is the private outdoor space created by removing a section of the damaged roof and creating a deck, a green wall of plants, and a second back entry.

RIGHT A wall of floor-to-ceiling glass windows separates the interior courtyard from the living spaces. The old hoist rail was used for moving bags of flour, feed, and seed to and from trains, cars, and trucks. Today it gives the room a distinct industrial character.

BOTTOM, LEFT The exterior of the old warehouse, now turned into urban loft residence, is Cheryl Morgan's home in Birmingham.

BOTTOM, MIDDLE The woodburning stove is a focal point of the sparsely decorated and spacious living area.

BOTTOM, RIGHT A sense of openness also defines the kitchen. Stainless steel appliances and countertops and painted brick reference the building's past life.

STUDIO GOODLIGHT AND LIESA COLE AND STAN BEDINGFIELD RESIDENCE

Birmingham is home base for photographer Liesa Cole and her husband, Stan Bedingfield. In 2015, they bought a building that became their professional studio and home. Architect Richard Carnaggio of CCR Architecture and Interiors added a second-floor residence, clad in cedar and charred in the Japanese technique shou sugi ban, to the old brick livery building below. Downstairs, an open airy space, is the photography studio, where separate sections are carved out—a bar for clients and spots for lounging. Upstairs is the living area with a kitchen, bedrooms, and a sitting room. The terraces on top of the building provide dramatic views of the city as well as access to light and air for the living spaces.

ABOVE An installation of Solatube units, which capture the daylight and bring it inside the building, also illuminates the rooftop of the building at night.

BELOW The entrance, with its bright blue door and steel facade, is hidden in a back alley in downtown Birmingham.

ABOVE At one end of the first floor is a skylight, and a three-story spiral staircase goes up to the residence and a terrace above.

BELOW The living room of the residence has a selection of mid-century modern furnishings and Liesa's photographs on display.

DAVID CARRIGAN RESIDENCE

When entrepreneur-restaurateur David Carrigan set out to build his own home, he chose architect Bruce Lanier. And why not—the two had worked together successfully on previous projects, one being David's pub, Carrigan's Public House, and the other was Brat Bröt (page 150). This conversion was as spectacular as the last, which transformed a plant nursery into a beer garden. Although the building was more conventional than the biergarten—an 1890s Kentucky Livery & Feed Supply warehouse near downtown—the views were stunning and the client's wish list, which included a swimming pool, was challenging. Lanier created a multilevel space that is linked with staircases made of reclaimed wood from the Carrigan's Public House project. Instead of closing off rooms with walls, all the spaces were made distinct, either through the materials used or how they were placed in relation to one another.

ABOVE This view of the former warehouse shows the new additions. The project started with only the brick shell of the building and its very deep steel girders according to Lanier.

RIGHT The second-floor swimming pool and bedroom balcony overlook an impressive cityscape of downtown Birmingham. The pool uses the original brick parapet as part of its coping.

ABOVE The elevated living room is defined by its white epoxy floors.

LEFT Efficiency is the defining element of the compact kitchen area, which also features elegant materials, such as the marble island.

WOODLAWN CYCLE CAFÉ

Initially, when it opened in 2016, Armand Margjeka's café in the emerging Birmingham neighborhood Woodlawn was a resting stop for fellow cyclists. A bike rack was incorporated into the dark-versus-light color decor scheme and mainly cycling races were shown on a giant television. But now the one-room 700-square-foot café, with its simple modern furniture made by Margjeka, who is also a musician, has become a gathering place for area residents and a destination for those seeking a European coffeehouse experience.

The bar's built-in cabinetry is painted a dark color and offsets the white tile floors and walls of the rest of the café.

ABOVE The Woodlawn Cycle Café building had many previous tenants, from a bicycle repair shop to a stone mason's shop, among others.

BELOW The dining area showcases furniture made from white oak by the owner-artist, Armand Margjeka.

NASHVILLE, TENNESSEE—MUSIC CITY—
home to country music, honkytonk, and
bluegrass. Nashville—Athens of the South—
home to twenty colleges and universities.
Nashville—state capital of Tennessee.
Nashville—Boomtown. Building cranes
populate the downtown skyline. Nashville
has access to at least three sectors of
Tennessee's economy—the music industry,
government, and manufacturing. The new
structures downtown are residential and
hospitality projects—built to accommodate
new residents and visitors alike. For
example, a new hotel from the Dream Hotel
Group and the Noelle hotel both opened in
2019. (Each one chose to convert an old
building into a new establishment.) At the
same time, there's a New Nashville with a
different vibe and understated aesthetic
thanks to the expansion of the visual arts
scene there. Sophistication and a sense
of whimsy are present in interior design
and major architectural renovations, such
as those made to the Frist Art Museum
building—a former post office. The city's
growth has been evolving for decades,
when like many other Southern cities, it
was deeply affected by the Civil War. Yet
Nashville has been reinventing itself,
building on innovation—for example, the
early car industry. Marathon Motor Works
had a factory there until 1914, so it
makes sense that Nissan built its first
US plant in nearby Smyrna in the 1980s,
based on the natural bedrock resources
there (among other factors). In the next
few years, an Amazon distribution center
will come to Nashville Yards, and that too
will bring change—more hotels and more
restaurants and more people.

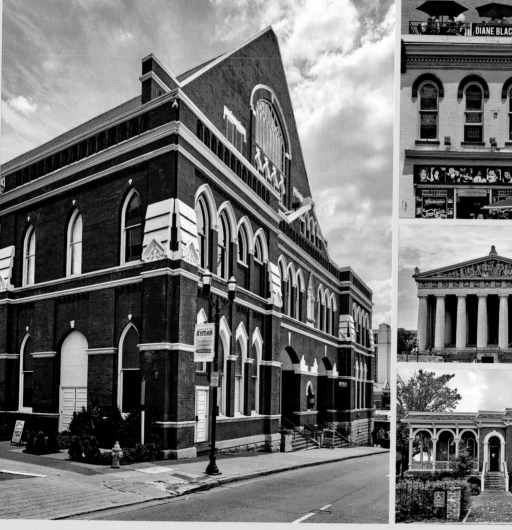

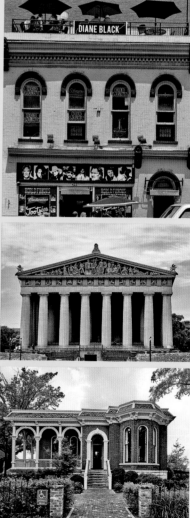

MARATHON VILLAGE

Little did Barry Walker know he was buying a part of Nashville history when in 1986 he purchased an abandoned building for his business's woodworking shop, in a rundown city neighborhood. But chance and a passion for historical research—some sections of the building dated from 1881 to 1908—led him to the story of the upstart automotive company, Marathon Motor Works, that used the buildings for manufacturing an early car, up until 1914. Walker developed the properties first as office spaces, then as commercial studios, and lately as retail shops and restaurants, designing a creative hub and revitalizing the area at the same time. As a tribute to the first owners, Walker established a small museum on the site and now has examples of the Marathon car along with other automotive collectibles.

ABOVE A 1912 touring car made by Marathon Motor Works, the first tenant, is on exhibit in the museum of Marathon Village.

BELOW An early Shell Oil gas station—part of Barry Walker's collection—is installed on the grounds of the village.

ABOVE Marathon Village is made up of multiple buildings that include the 32,000-square-foot administration building of the original owner, Marathon Motor Works car company.

BELOW One of the tenants of Marathon Village is Barista Parlor, a shop that is knowledgeable about specialty coffees.

FRIST ART MUSEUM

The Frist Art Museum's home is the 1930s main United States post office in Nashville. The restoration by architects Tuck-Hinton was completed in 2001. Many features of the original building—including the first post office's floor plan and interior materials, such as colored marble and cast aluminum detailing—were retained. Former offices and work areas were thoughtfully converted into galleries. The museum is also an excellent example of a visionary partnership, which included Thomas F. Frist Jr., MD, and his family, who saw a need for a visual arts center, and the City of Nashville, among other funders who bought the property and its grounds from the federal government.

TOP A postal cashier window from the 1930s was part of the restoration.

MIDDLE Cast aluminum grillwork was a feature of the old post office.

BOTTOM The museum is located near Union Station in the Gulch neighborhood of downtown Nashville. The building's architectural style has been described as both Classicism and Art Deco.

Visit
Martin
ArtQuest

Upper Level

ELEVATOR ↗

Nashville architects Marr and Holman designed the main post office during the Great Depression. A new grand staircase connects the first floor to the second-floor galleries.

The Grand Lobby of the Frist Art Museum retains many of the details of the former post office.

VADIS TURNER AND CLAY EZELL RESIDENCE

Vadis Turner and Clay Ezell were both originally from Nashville. So when they, along with their two children, felt squeezed out of Brooklyn, coming home was the next best thing. The move included buying a commercial building near downtown and transforming it (with the help of architect Nick Dryden and McClean Barbieri, an interior designer) into a colorful, expressive home. Turner is a successful artist and her keen sense of humor and knack for bright colors make their house unforgettable. What a creative place to grow up in.

RIGHT The former office building has three floors that include a terrace overlooking the thriving downtown scene. The red staircase entry gives a hint of the colorful interiors.

OPPOSITE The yellow staircase and bright paintings of the entranceway provide a bright welcome to the Turner-Ezell residence.

ABOVE A skylight overhead brightens the galley kitchen with its brick walls.

BELOW A painterly wallpaper by Pierre Frey is the focus of the family room, located just off the kitchen.

Comfortable seating areas are placed throughout the unconventional house, as are artworks, paintings, and sculptures by the homeowner.

DAVID LUSK GALLERY

Nashville isn't normally associated with white, minimalist spaces (color, and more color is the more recognized trend), but the David Lusk Gallery is part of a change in perception. It is also part of the thriving Wedgewood-Houston neighborhood, which has been revitalizing since at least 2016, when this gallery opened. The building was a truck mechanic's garage, hence the soaring, arched exposed ceilings and the glass garage door-like windows at the entry.

ABOVE The main gallery area holds regular exhibitions of contemporary and fine art. The polished cement floor is an elegant nod to its past use.

BELOW Light pours in through the front of the massive garage space, which also holds the works by artists the gallery represents among others.

ELEPHANT GALLERY AND STUDIO

Alex Lockwood, an artist, opened Elephant studio in 2016, and a year later, he opened the gallery. A pioneer in North Nashville, Lockwood has been part of the development of the Buchanan Arts District. The low-rise building with large windows on the street has a gallery space in front and studios in the back.

ABOVE A collaborative exhibition of paintings and objects by Dan Isaac Bortz and Lynnea Holland-Weiss titled *Faux Leisure* was featured in the gallery space.

BELOW A street view of Elephant Gallery with one of Brett Douglas Hunter's Aminals sculptures out front.

NOELLE,
NASHVILLE

The Noelle, Nashville, hotel is part of Marriott's signature portfolio of hospitality properties, but its building and interiors are unique to Nashville. According to the *Tennessean*, twenty new hotels opened in downtown Nashville between 2016 and 2019, and many of these newcomers have connections to the community—for example, the Dream Hotel nearby was designed by Meyer Davis Studio, whose partners are native Tennesseans. This hotel was also designed by locals, including architect Nick Dryden, who appreciated the history of the structure that had a previous life first as a hotel, in 1929, and more recently as a bank. Materials retained during the bank conversion, such as pink marble, terrazzo, and travertine, were restored and left in place.

LEFT Rich materials, such as leather on the furnishings and brass on the balconies' ornamental railings, are hallmarks of the restored interiors.

ABOVE The Trade Room of the Noelle hotel, with its low seating and arched windows, recalls an elegant era.

OPPOSITE The rooftop terrace with a view of Nashville's skyline is a new addition to the hotel.

OLD GLORY

In Edgehill Village, tucked away in a dark alley between old industrial warehouses and buildings, is a doorway painted with a yellow pyramid. One would never know the door leads to the coolest adaptive reuse project in Nashville. Owners and sisters Alexis Soler and Britt Soler took a nothing space that was left over from a dry cleaner next door and created a bar and restaurant that has a speakeasy feeling with a remarkable surprise—a 1920 boiler smokestack. Of course, new elements were added to make the space modern, comfortable, and intimate. Perhaps it's the scale of the stack against the bar below or the raw elements worked into the design that create the unique ambiance.

ABOVE You might miss the entry of Old Glory if you aren't in the know.

BELOW A new staircase is juxtaposed with the authentic materials of the old boiler room.

OPPOSITE The pièce de résistance or wow factor of the bar is the old boiler room's smokestack, which was stabilized and cleaned as part of the creation of the new bar and restaurant.

PITTTSB

PEN

STEEL BRIDGES PAINTED AZTEC GOLD—in honor of the Steelers football team—cross the Allegheny and Monongahela Rivers and connect Pittsburgh's downtown to the surrounding neighborhoods. It is here in the downtown that the seeds of Pittsburgh's transformation, from an industry of steel to a cultural dynamo, began and have spread and flourished. Institutions such as the Carnegie Museum of Art, founded in the late 19th century, have been the backbone of development in the 21st century, and not by accident. In the 1980s, philanthropists such as Jack Heinz recognized that the arts could drive an economic turnaround. Money was poured into the area, which in turn brought new businesses, galleries, and housing. And while Pittsburgh has long been associated with hard work and production, mainly from the steel industry, in recent years the shift is toward technology, with three of the big tech giants—Google, Microsoft, and Uber—having offices in town. The companies are there, profiting from the brain trust that is Carnegie Mellon University's student population, alumni, and faculty. Yet, culture is still giving the town its current cool ambiance. New dance companies, art spaces, bookstores, and restaurants are on the rise, and with good reason—it is affordable to start something new and be recognized. These small businesses are making Pittsburgh not only livable, but a destination that has driven its own comeback—which is not only concentrated downtown but throughout neighborhoods such as Lawrenceville and Troy Hill and nearby towns such as Braddock.

BOB BINGHAM STUDIO

Artist Bob Bingham has lived in Pittsburgh since 1989 and is a professor of art at Carnegie Mellon University. His artworks include installations that incorporate a variety of three-dimensional elements as well as site-specific environmental pieces that address the current state of natural resources. In the late 1980s, he was part of a group of artists who began restoring an 1899 building in the Old Duquense Brewery Complex for use as both studio and living space. His current studio is in a former manufacturing factory formally used by American Mine Safety Equipment company. Other artists rent space here, too, and Carnegie Mellon University's School of Drama is an anchor tenant. The studios have an abundance of natural light and fresh air that flows in through the multi-paned factory windows. Bingham's space has a wood shop as well as an open area where he is currently working on a long-term piece.

LEFT Bob Bingham is shown with one of his artworks in the background.

ABOVE Bingham's work in progress, titled *Still Life #9*, is on display in the studio space.

OPPOSITE The six-floor manufacturing building has approximately one-third of its spaces used by artists/tenants.

MATTRESS FACTORY

In 1975, artist Barbara Luderowski from Flushing, New York, bought an old Stearns & Foster mattress factory in Pittsburgh's Central Northside neighborhood for $10,000. Several years later, she and Pittsburgh native Michael Olijnyk cofounded the Mattress Factory with the mission to promote site-specific installation art, which at the time was a burgeoning art form and that oftentimes requires a lot of room for exhibition. Currently, permanent exhibits are mixed with temporary shows and the work of resident artists. Slowly, over the years, the museum has grown in an organic way, purchasing other buildings in the Mexican War Streets district and at the same time transforming a run-down, blighted place into a cultural center. "The reason the Mattress Factory is here," says Olijnyk, "is because we were here. We battled for everything. We lived through the successes and failures."

ABOVE A row house at 516 Sampsonia Way, around the corner from the original mattress factory, has been incorporated into the museum's programming. An exhibition artwork by Dennis Maher is shown in the newer space.

BELOW The Mattress Factory, a contemporary art center, is located in Pittsburgh's Central Northside neighborhood. A light sculpture titled *Acupuncture* by artist Hans Peter Kuhn is installed on the roof of the six-floor building.

ABOVE Yayoi Kusama's piece *Repetitive Vision* is permanently on view.

BELOW *Danaë* by James Turrell is also one of the museum's permanent exhibitions.

MICHAEL OLIJNYK RESIDENCE AT THE MATTRESS FACTORY

The top floor of the contemporary art museum the Mattress Factory is also the home of cofounders Michael Olijnyk and Barbara Luderowski, who lived there up until her death, in 2018. Although in 1977, local Victorian row houses surrounding the old mattress factory in the Mexican War Streets historic district were being restored, Luderowski and Olijnyk were the first to live in this industrial building. When they moved into the loft, there was no running water and their occupancy was illegal, but over the 40 years that they lived in the place, they amassed a collection of art, furniture, and objects that Olijnyk calls "a diary of our life together."

LEFT No space goes unfilled in the residence above the Mattress Factory, not even the kitchen of the loft.

OPPOSITE, BELOW A structural brick wall runs through the penthouse, dividing the space. Luderowski and Olijnyk made selections for the apartment together.

BELOW Display cases bulge with the sheer volume of objects, which include dolls, model cars of all sizes, cartoon characters figurines, dollhouses, and architectural models. Furniture of all styles and periods is also used throughout the apartment's sitting areas as well as in the dining area and kitchen.

Exposed pipes, brick walls, and steel doors are the backdrop to varied furnishings of the loft.

CITY OF ASYLUM

Diane Samuels and her husband, Henry Reese, started the Pittsburgh branch of the Cities of Asylum program in 2004. A nonprofit that began in Europe as a way to help writers who are threatened in their own countries, both physically and professionally, Cities of Asylum promotes free-speech protections. At the time, Samuels and Reese were living in Pittsburgh's North Side neighborhood, where they bought a row house nearby and offered a writer from China, Huang Xiang, a two-year residency. From there, the program grew to include public events such as readings and concerts. Nowadays, City of Asylum has a collection of buildings throughout the neighborhood as well as a garden. Their most recent purchase was a former Masonic Temple that has been turned into a cultural center, complete with a café, a bookstore, offices, and rooms for performances.

ABOVE Chinese poet Huang Xiang wrote one of his poems on the outside of his City of Asylum residence. This action started the tradition of asking artists to make text-based imagery on the exterior of the residence, which enlivens the alley where they are.

RIGHT *Pittsburgh-Burma House* by artist Than Htay Maung, who is the husband of City of Asylum resident writer Khet Mar, is part of the House Publications of City of Asylum.

OPPOSITE, ABOVE The Alphabet Reading Garden is part of City of Asylum's creative placemaking programming. The garden was designed by architect Joel Le Gall, artist Laura Jean McLaughlin, and artist and City of Asylum cofounder Diane Samuels. The garden has artworks made with images of alphabets.

OPPOSITE, BELOW A former Masonic Temple was turned into City of Asylum's cultural center.

ACE HOTEL

The Ace Hotel chain, based in Los Angeles, was one of the first hospitality groups to repurpose historic buildings as boutique hotels. The industry took notice, and today the Ace model is used throughout the United States. The restoration of the former YMCA in Pittsburgh's East Liberty community, a building that dates from 1909, was completed in 2015. On the ground floor, Ace opened a new restaurant with a local chef. Just down the hall, through the lobby, is an old gymnasium that has been given a new life as an event center and ballroom. Upstairs, the 63 rooms have totally modern updates—low beds and shaker pegs to hang clothes and towels. Local products from and in honor of Pittsburgh and Pennsylvania are the focus of the design throughout the hotel—the yellow and black tiles, for example, are a salute to the Steelers.

ABOVE The facade of the Ace Hotel still retains the signage of the YMCA, which used to occupy the building.

OPPOSITE, TOP LEFT Historic photographs are displayed above the marble-and-iron staircase.

OPPOSITE, TOP RIGHT A corner of the lobby restaurant, Whitfield, includes a fireplace with a marble surround as well as a shelving unit that does double duty as a serving station and a room divider.

OPPOSITE, BOTTOM The original gym with a running track that bisects the upper windows is now the ballroom of the hotel.

CLASS COMMUNITY SERVICE CENTRE

Community Living and Support Services (CLASS) is a nonprofit organization that provides services for people with disabilities of all kinds. The design of its Swissvale headquarters had to support its mission of accessibility for all within a structure that had been a grocery store and a children's play center. They turned to architect Paul Rosenblatt and his team at Springboard Design. At the beginning of the design process, the team met to discuss the key points of the space and what it needed to be for the 50 people who would use it for work and those visiting the space for classes. The first touchstone was a sense of openness—natural lighting was a priority, and then, of course, there were practical issues such as mobility—aisles and workstations needed to be wide. The materials chosen needed to be colorful—no institutional green here—as well as durable. All these elements came together to create a dynamic space that is accessible and LEED certified.

OPPOSITE Color was key to the renovation of the space. It is used throughout on walls and furnishings. The acoustical ceiling tiles float like a cloud about the workstations and hide the heating and cooling systems.

ABOVE The front facade of the Swissvale building is next to trolley tracks from the 1970s, a protected artifact of the city. The architects designed aluminum cladding, in contrast to the brick. A black staircase was also added and projects out to the exterior.

BELOW The breakroom café was moved to the front of the space. A yellow wall and wood ceiling and skylight make the room cheerful.

OMAHA, THE BIGGEST CITY IN NEBRASKA, is
known as home to Warren Buffett, Omaha Steaks,
and the Omaha Zoo, to name a few of its famous
residents, companies, and attractions. But
it is its midwestern location that made it a
major transportation hub in the early railroad
days. In the late 19th century, it also boasted
the world's largest stockyard, which created
a energetic city filled with busy commercial
districts. However, by the 1960s, the downtown
was in a state of flux, the warehouses sat
empty, and activity moved away from the center,
toward the suburbs. Business owners came up
with a plan to convert the buildings into the
Old Market, a walkable quartier filled with
shops, restaurants, galleries, and condominiums.
Today, it draws not only tourists but those who
want to experience an urban lifestyle in the
cafés by the cobblestone streets. The district
became a catalyst, and the adaptive reuse of
old buildings is expanding to other areas,
including the stockyard, where the Livestock
Exchange Building has been repurposed as
condominiums; North Omaha; and Benson. The IT
boom brought in technology and finance companies
such as Enron, Conagra, TD Ameritrade, and
Berkshire Hathaway. One consequence of the influx
is increased diversity, as more and different
kinds of families move to Omaha. In addition,
the art scene has a varied range, from world-
class art to architecture, on display at the
Joslyn Museum—whose first addition was British
architect Norman Foster's first building in
America, and their new addition will be designed
by Snøhetta and Alley Poyner Macchietto—and
at Japanese ceramic artist Jun Kaneko's Kaneko
art center.

HOWLIN' HOUNDS COFFEE

Greg Sechser's family owned a bar, the Diamond Bar on 16th, in downtown Omaha. Although he was interested in keeping the building—he lives upstairs with his two dogs—he wasn't interested in running a bar. Instead, he transformed the two street-level rooms into a coffee shop. The first space is the main room where the coffee is made and served. Sechser kept the original long bar with its now-vintage counter stools. The second room, connected via a brick archway, has been transformed by artist Gerard Pefung's bright, colorful murals, some of which are painted on plaster sections against the brick walls. The shop hosts events such as chess nights here, and tables and chairs give people a place to relax.

ABOVE Murals by Gerard Pefung enliven the seating areas of the coffee shop.

MIDDLE Greg Sechser, right, decided to keep the old bar from his family's first business and serve coffee there instead of drinks—definitely a change in program.

BELOW The former bar is on the ground level of this downtown building.

GALLERY 1516

Professional photographer Patrick Drickey opened the nonprofit Gallery 1516 in 2016, with a focus on exhibiting the work of regional Nebraska artists. For example, the gallery hosts the Nebraska Artist Biennial. The 19th-century brick stable had been turned into an equipment garage at the turn of the century and then later an Avis car garage. Renovations by BVH Architecture created a modern, spacious exhibition center, yet they also left evidence of the building's past life, by way of the wooden trusses above the gallery space.

ABOVE The wooden trusses from an early-20th-century remodel were preserved in the latest changes.

BELOW The exterior has a single large window and slatted wooden overhang above the entrance.

KANEKO

Started in 1998 by ceramic artist Jun Kaneko and his wife, Ree, the Kaneko is a nonprofit arts and cultural center located in the Old Market. Three early-20th-century warehouses—one was once an ice cream production site—make up the exhibition, performance, and education spaces of the center. Most recently, in 2016, a new entrance addition made of steel and glass, designed by Mark Mack Architects working with HDR Architecture, was added in order to connect the spaces and lead visitors through the galleries. The new atrium added almost 4,000 square feet to the organization's facilities.

ABOVE Part of the newly designed entry was a staircase to the upper offices and gallery areas.

BELOW The new entry was designed in harmony with the slope of the site. Large front windows allow visitors to have a preview of exhibitions installed in the galleries.

ABOVE The arched trusses of the exposed ceiling add to the expansive scale of the exhibition spaces. Exhibitions are both rotating and ongoing.

BELOW Jun Kaneko's own large ceramic sculptures are also on view.

STEVE AND JULIE BURGESS RESIDENCE

The building in North Omaha was a 4,000-square-foot die works shop in 1915. It was the first building on the block of the then up-and-coming neighborhood. Steve and Julie Burgess, whose family had owned the property since the 1930s and had an active business within the same block, only recently decided to renovate. They were looking to downsize and to create an urban loft lifestyle. The renovation was completed by Geoff DeOld and Emily Andersen of DeOld Andersen Architecture in 2018. The architects opened up the lower half of the brick facade, adding a laser-cut steel screen that was designed by Steve and was inspired by decorative screens of the Middle East. The steel wall creates an inner courtyard between the sidewalk and the loft's entry. Other interventions included a roof deck and skylights throughout to bring light into the rooms.

ABOVE The two-story structure has been in the family for more than 70 years. The black laser-cut wall adds a modern design feature.

BELOW A glimpse through the living area and the glass window walls to the laser-cut steel facade.

OPPOSITE The kitchen, with two large windows and a skylight, is in the back of the first floor.

MARIA FERNANDEZ RESIDENCE

In 2014, Maria Fernandez decided to move from her suburban home in Council Bluffs, Iowa, to the Old Market. It was a neighborhood that she knew well, as she had owned an Indian restaurant there for many years. The 1,700-square-foot space was an empty loft in an industrial warehouse. Fernandez tapped her son, architect Rajiv Fernandez, to design her new home. Layers of opacity increase toward the interior of the two-bedroom space. An avid collector, Maria has artworks, antiques, and modern furnishings on display throughout her home.

ABOVE The living room with multiple seating areas was designed to be close to the two-story-high windows.

LEFT This view through the loft from the living area shows the kitchen, the mezzanine, and the entry.

OPPOSITE White walls at either end of the living room offer exhibition space for Maria Fernandez's art collection.

BOILER ROOM
RESTAURANT

Sam Mercer, who was responsible for the development of the Old Market neighborhood, also opened a restaurant and bar there—the Boiler Room. Just as its name implies, the space in an old warehouse was once a boiler room of the Bemis Bag building. Today, the original mezzanine is a dining room that overlooks the subterranean bar and open kitchen.

ABOVE Authentic elements such as the exposed wood ceiling, brick walls, and iron railings give the space its sense of warmth and character.

BELOW The Boiler Room's sidewalk café is located just outside the main restaurant.

OPPOSITE With two levels, both the food and drink enthusiast can be accommodated. Wine is stored under the staircase. Dinner is enjoyed upstairs.

TODD SIMON
RESIDENCE

Todd Simon's house has a nickname—the Art House—
and one can see why when greeted at the front entrance,
where a Jun Kaneko vessel is placed in a glass vitrine.
Inside the modern abode, which was designed by Jeffrey
Dolezal of TACKarchitects Inc., Simon's extensive
collection of contemporary art is on full display, not only
in the upstairs living quarters but also in the specially
designed gallery below the main level. A white cube—
almost an artwork itself—floats in the space and holds
the bar, kitchen, and shelving for the display of art
objects, not to mention the electrical and mechanical
elements for the open living room. The house is up-to-
date with geothermal heating and cooling systems, LED
lighting, and other energy-saving features. Porticos on
the exterior help to regulate the sunlight and therefore
the heating of the interior spaces.

OPPOSITE, ABOVE A painting by Callum Innes is hung above a stairwell to the gallery.

OPPOSITE, BELOW The below-ground gallery holds large artworks and paintings from Simon's personal collection. On the ledge is a sculpture by Claudia Alvarez.

ABOVE A white cube is at the nexus of the living room, dining room and kitchen. The cedar wall extends from the exterior through the interior living spaces.

BELOW The swimming pool and terrace is accessible from the living room and dining area. The low-level modern house is clad in cedar and aluminum.

A Nick Cave Soundsuit is placed in the upstairs living area among other artworks by Heron Bassett, on the floor, and by Vik Muniz near the pool table.

DEN
COLORA

A GOLD RUSH FIRST BROUGHT settlers to the Denver area in the 1860s. Evidence of those early boom days still exists—for example, the Brown Palace Hotel, designed by architect Frank E. Edbrooke, which wows visitors with its seven-floor atrium lobby, opened in 1892. Part of the draw was, and is, the location of the city. Denver sits on a high plateau at the base of the Rocky Mountains. Today, the outdoor lifestyle of biking, hiking, and walking are an integral part of the city. The revitalization of Denver's downtown started in the late 1980s with the plan to create a walkable, livable neighborhood, more than the business center it had become, which catered to the oil and gas industries. The changes that city officials and preservationists worked together to implement included renovating and repurposing existing historic structures. Neighborhoods such as RiNo, short for River North, and LoDo, which stands for Lower Downtown, were rezoned and developed to include microbreweries, restaurants, and residential living. The RiNo business improvement district worked to make the area friendly to artists, supporting the CRUSH mural festival to activate the walls of the old warehouses and to create a destination. Today, it is possible to take the light-rail service from Denver International Airport into Lower Downtown and arrive at the old Union Station. It is a journey of contrasts—traveling from the modern airport to the old train station. The original station was built in the 1880s and was reopened after extensive renovation in 2014 to include restaurants, a boutique hotel, a bookstore, several bars, and a brewpub.

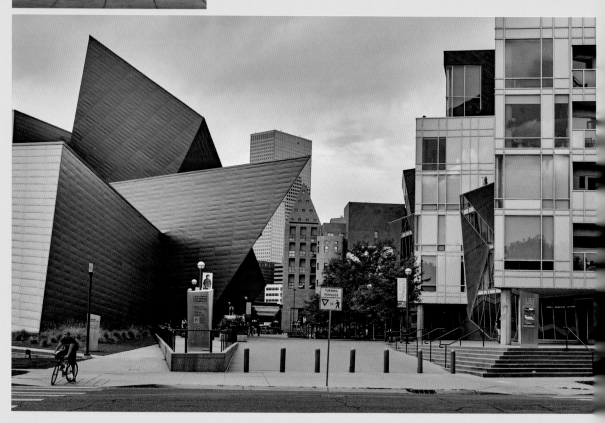

UNION STATION

To say that Union Station is a busy hub is an understatement. There have been major renovations and reconstructions of the structure since the station first opened in 1881. The design of how and which trains and buses come in and out of the station has also changed. Most recently, light-rail service to and from the new Denver Airport begins and ends at the terminal, and it is the depot for all Denver's bus service. Not only that, the building is the home to restaurants, shops, an independent bookstore, and the Crawford Hotel, named in honor of preservationist Dana Crawford, who worked to transform the area, making this transportation center the heart of Denver's Lower Downtown Historic District revitalization and a major piece of Denver's urbanization puzzle.

BELOW The new open-air train platform is next to the Historic Union Station.

ABOVE The renovation of the train station, which reopened in 2014, included the preservation of the five arched windows of the 66-foot-high waiting room. The Cooper Lounge is located on the mezzanine above the Terminal Bar.

BELOW Restaurants, bars, and the Crawford Hotel surround the waiting area of the train station, known as the Great Hall, which is set up with dining tables, seating areas, and game tables and is open to the public.

The canopy of the train hall that serves the Union Station Commuter Rail system.

THE SOURCE HOTEL
AND MARKET HALL

The Source Hotel and Market Hall is a unique combination in the River North Arts District (also known as RiNo). First, the Market Hall, an 1880 foundry building of the Colorado Iron Works company, has been repurposed as a food hall with gourmet-food purveyors as well as restaurants and bars. In warmer weather, tables spill out into the courtyard, creating a romantic evening experience. And then there is the 100-room Source Hotel, along with its high-end shops and art gallery, which sits on the edge of busy Brighton Boulevard. Inside, the old building is connected to the hypermodern hotel through an addition, and outside, the buildings are connected through a series of ramps and walkways. The fluidity between the old and the new spaces feels seamless even if the two buildings are strikingly different.

ABOVE The two brick buildings of the Market Hall are physically located next door to the modern hotel but are miles apart in design style.

BELOW The Source Hotel was designed by Dynia Architects and opened in 2013.

IL POSTO

ABOVE Over 100 handblown Bocci light fixtures float above the elegant dining room.

BELOW Il Posto opened on a corner in the RiNo neighborhood in 2017. Both doors and windows swivel open in temperate weather.

The challenge for the architects at LIVstudio was how to take an established Italian restaurant with a loyal following, Il Posto, and inject a similarly dynamic personality into its new home in a former 3,000-square-foot warehouse. Luckily, the building had already been designed by Tres Birds Workshop and was waiting for the right tenant. Tres Birds had planned several smart interventions in the cavernous space—first, adding a mezzanine and upper balcony that have views of downtown Denver and the main restaurant below, and then inserting large floor-to-ceiling windows/doors that pivot open like sails on a ship to the L-shaped patio outside, which takes advantage of the corner location to create a relationship with the neighborhood. Inside, LIVstudio then installed the large circular banquettes that are almost rooms within themselves, and double-height shelving for wine storage and display that also serves as a room divider.

DENVER CENTRAL MARKET

The 1920s building that now contains the Denver Central Market, a food hall and market, had several past lives, including as a novelty company and an antique automobile showroom. The exposed-brick walls, high ceilings, and natural light from the front wall of windows of the old building, as well as the newly installed ceramic tile flooring, all contribute to the authentic ambience of the place. Eleven vendors, including a butcher shop, a bakery, a coffee shop, and a chocolatier, each with its own design identity, make the room feel full, busy, and welcoming. Wood tables and chairs are placed among the stations, so visitors can stay to enjoy their purchases and take in the aromas and atmosphere. The market is part of developers Ken Wolf and Ari Stutz's plan to bring a food destination to the RiNo neighborhood, formerly a commercial warehouse district.

ABOVE The open dining area is surrounded by a mix of vendors, such as Culture Meat & Cheese and the Local Butcher. The space among the shops is easily navigated. LIVstudio, which has designed other RiNo projects with the developer, also worked on the market.

ABOVE The brick columns of the exterior of the Denver Central Market were preserved along with its arched glass windows and entry.

BELOW Crema Bodega's counter is made with reclaimed wood.

FAMILY JONES
SPIRIT HOUSE

Architect Michael M. Moore of Tres Birds Workshop
brings his artistic vision and sensibilities to the Family
Jones Spirit House, a distillery located in a mainly residential neighborhood, Lower Highlands. The architect
added a two-story extension and terrace to a former
low-rise tattoo parlor. The extension of the tasting room
juts out beyond the original building toward the sidewalk,
and its narrow vertical front windows call attention to
the place, especially at night, when it glows as a lantern
would. The interiors of the cocktail lounge have dramatic
features and a mix of textures of materials throughout—
from the walls' stones, some of which appear to have
been pulled out to create opportunities for display, to
the dark blue velvet of the low seating, which allows an
unimpeded view of the cityscape.

ABOVE On the facade, fin-like wooden slats between
the windows are set against the other materials used
on-site, such as steel, glass, and stone.

BELOW The building has been subtly integrated into
the neighborhood. At night, the cocktail lounge appears
to be a residential living room rather than a bar.

ABOVE A large copper still floats above the bar and anchors the design of the distillery's cocktail lounge, which serves its own spirits, such as gin, bourbon, rye, and vodka.

BELOW During the day, the front windows offer a view of downtown Denver.

AUSTIN, TEXAS, IS A VIBRANT CITY. It is full of music, from the songbird that wakes you up, to the lone guitar player strumming for tips on the sidewalk, to artists at an outdoor concert organized for the South by Southwest Music Festival in the evening. For many, music is the first association with the town—the television show *Austin City Limits* has been broadcast nationally on PBS since 1975. Austin is also full of art. An installation titled *Uplifted Ground* by Michael Singer Studio greets arrivals at the Austin-Bergstrom International Airport, and a sculpture titled *Forever Bicycles* by Ai Weiwei was placed beside a hiking and biking trail. Austin is the site for Ellsworth Kelly's *Austin*, the artist's only built project. The University of Texas is based in Austin. The city has been the capital of the state government since 1844. However lately, the city is associated with technology. It's transforming from a funky, affordable place to a center of enterprise as some of the biggest companies in the industry set up operations here—Google and Apple being just two. As a result, Austin is rebuilding to accommodate the growth, which has led to an influx of new residents. In fact, "the whole city is being repurposed," says architect Ben Dimmitt. This reboot is causing anxiety among longtime locals about the impact it will have on housing, on traffic, and on their laid-back, often self-described "weird" lifestyle, as well as on all the things that made Austin cool in the first place—the combination of history, culture, education, access to the outdoors, and the food scene.

SEAHOLM
POWER PLANT

Seaholm Power Plant sat empty for almost 20 years. During that time, there was a lot of speculation about what would happen to the site, given its history and prominent location. The city-owned facility was built in the 1950s and it had been a major source of power for the city. Preservationists stepped in to help save the structure, and in 2005, the city called for proposals for the redevelopment of the site. As a result of those efforts, the plant was transformed into office spaces, yet the structural aspects of the original concrete building, with its various stacks and exposed ductwork, remained intact. A plaza was created behind the plant, with new buildings surrounding it. The new construction include a residential tower with restaurants on the street level as well as retail shops and a grocery store. A whole neighborhood has blossomed from the once-derelict plant.

ABOVE The old power plant was restored and sections were left open for the public to view and visit.

BELOW The west entry still has the original signage.

ABOVE A plaza with green space connects the three buildings of the mixed-use site.

BELOW Artists Josef Kristofoletti and Sten & Lex were commissioned to create a mural titled *Accordion16* along a wall next to the power station.

The three smokestacks of the power plant were incorporated into the new development. The area around the former power plant is now known as the Seaholm District.

Athenahealth
The Generator

True Food Kitchen
Seaholm Residences
Nekter Juice Bar

Healthy Pet
Trader Joe's
Ruiz Salon
Optique
Baked Bear
Toothbar

THE CONTEMPORARY AUSTIN

The Contemporary Austin is an art museum specializing in contemporary art, with two locations. The Jones Center is located on Congress Avenue in downtown Austin, and the other site, Laguna Gloria, is about five miles from the downtown center. Since being built more than 100 years ago, the Jones Center building had been a theater and a department store. Paul Lewis of LTL Architects was responsible for the initial transformation into an art center and also the renovation that took place in 2016. Today, the museum is among the institutions and commercial galleries that make up a vital and international art scene in Austin.

ABOVE The museum's Jones Center takes advantage of its corner location on Congress Avenue to exhibit artwork such as Jim Hodges's sculpture *With Liberty and Justice for All (A Work in Progress)*, which is permanently installed along the roof-deck terrace.

OPPOSITE The Contemporary Austin's Museum Without Walls program worked in partnership with the Waller Creek Conservancy to bring artist Ai Weiwei's *Forever Bicycles* to the Waller Creek Delta, a public park. The work was on display from 2017 to 2019.

AUSTIN BY ELLSWORTH KELLY

In 1986, artist Ellsworth Kelly designed a simple white building for a client and incorporated his signature primary-color scheme, which distinguishes his paintings, drawings, and prints. Yet for over 30 years, the project remained unbuilt. Then as good luck would have it, the Blanton Museum of Art on the University of Texas at Austin campus agreed to take on the fundraising and the production to complete the project. By this time, Kelly was in his 90s and the work turned out to be his last piece. He died just when construction began. The chapel-like structure is filled with Kelly's work, which takes on a meditative presence as light flows through the stained-glass windows, of different colors, which Kelly designed.

TOP Kelly's totem-like sculpture and a series of black-and-white marble panels, all the same size, are installed inside.

ABOVE *Austin* by Ellsworth Kelly found a home on the campus of the University of Texas at Austin.

OPPOSITE A view of one of the three stained-glass windows by Ellsworth Kelly.

CENTRAL LIBRARY, AUSTIN PUBLIC LIBRARY

A soaring six-floor atrium and breezy rooftop garden with panoramic views of Lady Bird Lake and downtown are hallmarks of the Central Library of Austin's public library system. These features also enhance a sense of openness that brings the community together in this enormous building of just under 200,000 square feet, all of which accommodates a variety of flexible spaces, from library stacks, to children's play areas, to a 350-seat forum and reading rooms. The design of Austin's Central Library was a joint project between two architectural firms, Lake Flato and Shepley Bulfinch. The two companies worked together to create an innovative structure that incorporates environmentally conscious systems such as rainwater harvesting and an in-ground cistern.

ABOVE AND RIGHT Wide walkways beneath the floors of the library promote walking and cycling to the library entrance.

OPPOSITE Perforated anodized aluminum panels and Lueders limestone are part of the facade.

ABOVE The six-story atrium links the floors of the library with a series of staircases in a variety of materials. The giant stairwell is also a lightwell that provides natural light to all the levels.

OPPOSITE Transparency, light, and air were key concepts of the library's design.

GARAGE

William Ball and his two business partners, Bron Hager and
Connor Oman, took on the renovation of a unique room within
Austin's first 1950 drive-in bank—the American National Bank
that opened in 1954. Customers would pull into the garage,
where a valet would park their car while they completed transac-
tions within the Florence Knoll–designed interiors. The bank was
the height of mid-century modern business. An almost forgotten
space, the valet's station has been transformed into Garage cocktail bar. It's a room with a cool mood, mainly because the original
materials were preserved in the construction and enhanced in the
transformation. For example, the main circular bar references the
round windows of the office station. In addition, the slanted concrete roof, the low tables and chairs, a muted color palette, and
curved leather banquettes create intimate effects. Sipping a craft
cocktail while taking in the textures of the jewel box–like space is
a unique and sophisticated experience.

ABOVE An overall view of the room includes
the central bar and discreet banquettes and
seating areas.

LEFT The original entry was preserved along
with the celadon-colored tiles.

OPPOSITE You might miss the entrance of
Garage cocktail lounge if not for its simple,
straightforward signage.

979 SPRINGDALE
IN EAST AUSTIN

979 Springdale is a mixed-use development in East Austin. A series of former food-distribution warehouses, it was filled with blue shelving from floor to ceiling. Architect Jamie Chioco had the idea to flip the inside out. Using the already blue steel shelving, he created a modern screen and portico that instantly call attention to the building's facade and patio, which is used by a brewpub and restaurant. Around the corner, planters with seating were designed for the interior courtyard and painted a similar blue. The buildings have a range of tenants, from a fitness center to tech companies to the Rise coffee shop, who converted a trailer into a coffee bar.

ABOVE Rise coffee bar sets up in the courtyard of 979 Springdale.

BELOW The blue color permeates the design, as planters with space for seating also used the color.

OPPOSITE Blue shelving was used as exterior building material to create a colorful entry to the former warehouses.

MA

RFA
TEXAS

MARFA, TEXAS, POPULATION JUST BELOW 2,000,

is well-known as the town that art saved. When the military moved out in the 1940s, the Lone Star State town suffered. Thirty years later, the artist Donald Judd was driving around the Southwest looking for an escape from the New York City art world when he stopped in Marfa. The destiny of the town was changed forever. He bought buildings to use as his studio and living space. With help from the Dia Art Foundation, he was able to purchase the abandoned Fort D. A. Russell and transform it into a permanent installation of not only his artwork but that of other artists, such as Dan Flavin and Robert Irwin. These days, buildings throughout the town have been repurposed as innovative art galleries, casual restaurants, and chic retail shops. The small adobe houses have been renovated and upgraded. The redesigns take cues from vernacular architecture, with details such as corrugated steel roofs, polished cement flooring, and adobe clay. The desert palette—soft yellows of the grasses, pale reds of the earth, bright blues of the wide-open sky—is used throughout the town. Judd's minimalist vision has made an impact on the town's aesthetic. On the main street, buildings are painted bright white and rust abounds. The new economy relies on tourism but also suffers from rising property taxes. Yet Marfa is described as the best small town by those who live there. They remark on a combination of pleasant climate, an influx of young civic-minded residents, and the world-class culture.

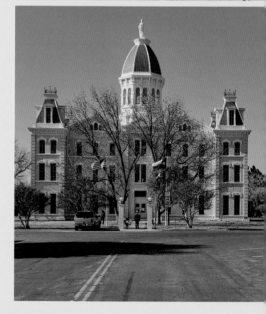

BARBARA HILL
RESIDENCE

Somehow a four-room house is enough. There are no shortcuts, and everything is included—a living room, a dining room, a bedroom, a kitchen, a bath. How does designer Barbara Hill do it? Years spent as a professional, designing projects for clients and herself, have paid off. She knows the right combination of "less is more" (as in the minimal gray sofa positioned against a sitting room/ dining room wall) and when more is more (art that is placed throughout, and in every nook and cranny). This casita, parts of which were built before the turn of the century, isn't her first Marfa project, and surely won't be her last.

ABOVE The living room area of the tiny house has a minimal design, with most of the furnishing being white.

ABOVE The little white house on the left, owned by designer
Barbara Hill, has been restored as her Marfa residence.

BELOW The back bedroom has a double height ceiling
and an inset ledge for displaying personal memorabilia.

The dining room has a corner fireplace and a print of Andy Warhol's Elvis portrait as its focal point.

WRONG GALLERY

Buck Johnson and her husband, artist Camp Bosworth, came to Marfa 18 years ago. They opened the Wrong Store and Gallery in 2009, in what was the first church in Marfa. The large pointed-arch glass window in the front is a remnant. The gallery has a flow of artwork, both on exhibit and available for sale, on a table in the middle of the space. The gallery was moved to a new location in 2019. The business card reads "the customer is always Wrong." Johnson has curated a similar sense of humor.

ABOVE The interior of the Wrong Gallery, a former church, has both white floors and walls. Artworks seem to float in the space.

BELOW A large plate glass pointed arch gothic style window—a hold-over from the church—brings light into the Wrong Gallery. The giant neon orange horseshoe is a gallery signpost.

BALLROOM MARFA

Ballroom Marfa is a cultural space that was created from a former dance hall. The gallery hosts art shows along with musical performances and other events. Virginia Lebermann and Fairfax Dorn started the nonprofit in 2003. It has taken center stage in Marfa's art world by supporting artists and their unconventional works. The bright white building is a beacon on the main highway that runs through the small town— it is hard to miss its bright blue signage.

ABOVE As seen from the road, the Marfa Ballroom's design is modern yet minimal.

BELOW The simple lines of the old dance hall are also evident from the side parking lot as well.

THE CHINATI FOUNDATION/ LA FUNDACIÓN CHINATI

Founded by Donald Judd in 1978 as a permanent art installation of his work and the work of other artists, the Chinati Foundation/La Fundación Chinati site opened in 1986 on the grounds of a former military base. Judd, with financial help from the Dia Art Foundation, worked to develop the program for the museum. It includes installations by artists such as Robert Irwin and Dan Flavin, Judd's friends. One of the most recent installations is by Irwin, who conceived an untitled art piece on the footprint of the old hospital. Walking along the visitors' path, from one end of the site through Judd's sculptures installed in the Texas landscape, is a transforming experience. Judd's work in relation to the natural environment, placed as the artist wished, creates an environment like no other.

A former military barrack holds Donald Judd's *100 untitled works in mill aluminum, 1982-1986.*

TOP   Robert Irwin's 2016 installation was built on the footprint of the old army hospital on the base.

OPPOSITE   The interior of the event center has furniture designed by Judd as well. The artist used this space for entertaining visitors to the foundation.

ABOVE   A doorway designed by Judd leads to the event center on the Chinati campus.

The u-shaped barracks of the military base are
now exhibition spaces for work by artists such as
Dan Flavin and Ilya Kabakov.

SELECTED BIBLIOGRAPHY

Florida, Richard. "What Draws Creative People? Quality of Place." *Urbanland*, October 12, 2012. https://urbanland .uli.org/industry-sectors/what-draws -creative-people-quality-of-place/

Lerner, Michele. "The New Boomtowns: Why More People are Relocating to 'Secondary' Cities." *Washington Post*, November 8, 2018. https:// www.washingtonpost.com/realestate /the-new-boomtowns-why-more -people-are-relocating-to-secondary -cities/2018/11/07/f55f96f4-d618 -11e8-aeb7-ddcad4a0a54e_story.html

Wong, Liliane. *Adaptive Reuse: Extending the Lives of Buildings*. Basel, Switzerland: Birkhäuser Verlag GmbH, 2017.

NORTH ADAMS, MASSACHUSETTS
Emerson, Linda. "The promise of MASS MoCA." *Commonwealth Magazine*, July 11, 2017. https:// commonwealthmagazine.org/arts-and -culture/the-promise-of-mass-moca/

McKeough, Tim. "Betting on the Berkshires." *New York Times*, April 13, 2018. https://www.nytimes.com/2018 /04/13/realestate/second-homes -berkshires.html

Smith, Roberta. "MASS MoCA: It's a Site for All Eyes." *New York Times*, June 15, 2017. https://www.nytimes .com/2017/06/15/arts/design /mass-moca-its-a-site-for-all-eyes .html?searchResultPosition=4

Sprague, John L. *87 Marshall Street Creation, Disruption, and Renewal in the Northern Berkshires*. Williamstown, Massachusetts: John Sprague, 2016.

GREENVILLE, SOUTH CAROLINA
Huff Jr., Archie Vernon. *Greenville: The History of the City and County in the South Carolina Piedmont*. Columbia, South Carolina: University of South Carolina Press, 1995.

Bruss, Kelley. "Greenville's Old Mills Forge New Paths." *Greenville News*, April 19, 2016. https://www .greenvilleonline.com/story/insider /extras/2016/04/19/greenvilles-old -mills-forge-new-paths/83230136/

Grem, Darren. "Brandon Mill." *South Carolina Encyclopedia*, May 17, 2016.

http://www.scencyclopedia.org/sce /entries/brandon-mill/

BUFFALO, NEW YORK
Buffalo Rising. "Up close with Joe Cascio-Northland Workforce Training Center and Gigi's Restaurant." *Buffalo Uprising*, February 4, 2019. https:// www.buffalorising.com/2019/02/up -close-with-photographer-joe-cascio -northland-workforce-training-center -and-gigis-restaurant/

LaChiusa, Chuck. "Exterior-Standard Grain Elevator." *Buffalo as an Architectural Museum*. 2013. https:// buffaloah.com/a/stclair/1/ext.html

Lange, Alexandra. "A Buffalo Case Study: Can Architecture Bring a City Back?" Curbed, August 6, 2015. https:// www.curbed.com/2015/8/6/9933782 /alexandra-lange-buffalo-architecture -preservation

Ouroussoff, Nicolai. "Saving Buffalo's Untold Beauty." *New York Times*, November 14, 2008. https://www .nytimes.com/2008/11/16/arts /design/16ouro.html

Neufeld, Lesley. *Frank Lloyd Wright's Martin House Complex*. Buffalo, New York: Martin House Restoration Corporation, 2004 (Updated text 2010).

Sisson, Patrick. "How Buffalo Turned Architectural Heritage into an Engine for Reinvention." Curbed, June 28, 2017. https://www.curbed.com/2017/6/28 /15887962/buffalo-architecture-frank -lloyd-wright-louis-sullivan

OAKLAND, CALIFORNIA:
Gassman, Gary. "7 Reasons to Visit This California Town Right Now." *Architectural Digest*, November 28, 2017. https://www.architecturaldigest.com /story/oakland-california-travel-guide

Haber, Matt. "Oakland: Brooklyn by the Bay." *New York Times*, May 2, 2014. https://www.nytimes.com/2014/05/04 /fashion/oakland-california-brooklyn -by-the-bay.html

Kimmelman, Michael. "Design as Balm for a Community's Soul." *New York Times*, October 10, 2012. https://www .nytimes.com/2012/10/11/arts/design /tassafaronga-village-and-richardson -apartments-in-bay-area.html

Stoughton, John. "Cutting-edge 3D Printing Pushes Construction Boundaries in an Oakland cabin." *Architect's Newspaper*, March 12, 2018. https:// archpaper.com/2018/03/cutting-edge -3d-printing-pushes-construction -berkeley/#gallery-0-slide-0

PORTLAND, OREGON
Pollack, Naomi R. "Common Ground: A Master Recreates His Homeland's Aura in a Verdant American Setting." *Architectural Record*, August 1, 2017. https://www.architecturalrecord.com /articles/12872-portland-japanese -garden-cultural-village-by-kengo -kuma-associates

Sokol, David. "Swift Agency by BeeBe Skidmore Architects." *Architectural Record*, April 1, 2017. https://www .architecturalrecord.com/articles /12468-swift-agency-by-beebe -skidmore-architects

von Hagen, Bettina et al., editors. *Rebuilt Green: The Natural Capital Center and the Transformative Power of Building*. Portland, Oregon: Ecotrust, 2003.

CINCINNATI, OHIO
Glusac, Elaine. "36 Hours in Cincinnati." *New York Times*, August 17, 2017. https://www.nytimes.com/interactive /2017/08/17/travel/what-to-do-36 -hours-in-cincinnati-ohio.html

Morgan, Michael D. *Over-the-Rhine: When Beer Was King*. Charleston, SC: The History Press, 2010.

Muschamp, Herbert. "ART/ ARCHITECTURE; Zaha Hadid's Urban Mothership." *New York Times*, June 8, 2003. https://www.nytimes.com/2003 /06/08/arts/art-architecture-zaha -hadid-s-urban-mothership.html

Over-the-Rhine architecture. (n.d.) http://www.otrfoundation.org/OTR _Architecture.htm

Schneider, Keith. "Downtown Cincinnati Thrives as Riot's Memories Recede." *New York Times*, February 24, 2015. https://www.nytimes.com/2015/02/25 /realestate/cincinnatis-downtown-finds -a-path-forward.html

RICHMOND, VIRGINIA

Hermanson, Marissa. "A Historic U.S. Post Office Is Transformed into a Digital Agency's New Modern Office." *Dwell*, August 27, 2017. https://www.dwell.com/article/a-historic-u.s.-post-office-is-transformed-into-a-digital-agencys-new-modern-office-84588ff6

Kollatz Jr., Harry. "The Curve Around the Station." *Richmond Magazine*, December 23, 2013. https://richmondmagazine.com/news/richmond-history/I-95-cross-into-Shockoe/

Schneider, Gregory S. "Richmond's New Civil War Museum Aims to Shatter Conventional views of the Conflict." *Washington Post*. April 26, 2019 https://www.washingtonpost.com/local/virginia-politics/richmonds-new-civil-war-museum-aims-to-shatter-conventional-views-of-the-conflict/2019/04/26/f0b7e7ce-6785-11e9-a1b6-b29b90efa879_story.html

Slipek, Edwin. "Countdown to Launch." *Style Weekly*, April 10, 2018. https://www.styleweekly.com/richmond/countdown-to-launch/Content?oid=8217197

BIRMINGHAM, ALABAMA

Kwak, Chaney. "36 Hours in Birmingham, Ala." *New York Times*, June 15, 2017. https://www.nytimes.com/interactive/2017/06/15/travel/what-to-do-36-hours-in-birmingham-alabama.html

Whitely, Carla Jean. "How 750 miles of trails are connecting Birmingham." *Birmingham Magazine*, June 11, 2018. https://www.al.com/bhammag/2018/06/how_750_miles_of_trails_are_co.html

Nawab, Akhtar. "A Chef's Tour of the Best Restaurants in Birmingham." *Fathom*, November 9, 2017. https://fathomaway.com/best-restaurants-birmingham-alabama/

Scheffler, Daniel. "How Best to Spend a Weekend in Birmingham, the South's 'Magic City'." *Vogue*, October 26, 2017. https://www.vogue.com/article/weekend-guide-birmingham-alabama

NASHVILLE, TENNESSEE

Evanoff, Ted. "How Tennessee Became Car County, USA." *Commercial Appeal*, February 28, 2019. https://www.commercialappeal.com/story/money/cars/2018/02/28/tennessee-auto-industry-nissan-smyrna-gm-spring-hill-volkswagen-chattanooga/1028963001/

Kurutz, Steven. "Taking Brooklyn to Nashville." *New York Times*, May 4, 2017. https://www.nytimes.com/2017/05/04/style/taking-brooklyn-to-nashville.html

Lombard, Stefan. "Old Factories Made New." *Hagerty*, February 6, 2015. https://www.hagerty.com/articles-videos/articles/2015/02/06/old-factories-made-new

Mazza, Sandy. "Nashville's Hotel Fever: How Many Is Too Many?" *Tennessean*, January 31, 2019. https://www.tennessean.com/story/money/2019/01/31/hotel-nashville-tourism-real-estate-investment/2666998002/

Vora, Shivani. "Five Places to Go in Nashville." *New York Times*, March 1, 2018. https://www.nytimes.com/2018/03/01/travel/five-places-to-go-in-nashville-wedgewood-houston.html

PITTSBURGH, PENNSYLVANIA

Bannan, Jennifer. "Forging Urban Frontiers." *Carnegie Mellon Today*, February 29, 2016. https://www.cmu.edu/cmtoday/artsculture_innovation/urban-revitalization-pittsburgh/

Heyman, Stephen. "How Pittsburgh Quietly Became a Culture Capital." *Departures*, September 19, 2017. https://www.departures.com/travel/pittsburgh-culture-things-to-do

Russo, John. "The Pittsburgh Conundrum." *American Prospect*, July 26, 2017, https://prospect.org/labor/pittsburgh-conundrum/

OMAHA, NEBRASKA

Peterson, Lucas. 'In Omaha, a Progressive Approach to Free Time." *New York Times*, October 3, 2018. https://www.nytimes.com/2018/10/03/travel/frugal-omaha.html

Sachs, Andrea. "You're going *where*? Omaha." *Washington Post*, June 7, 2017. https://www.washingtonpost.com/graphics/lifestyle/vacation-ideas/things-to-do-in-omaha/?noredirect=on

Omaha Magazine Staff. "Historic Buildings of the Old Market." *Omaha Magazine*, October 3, 2014. https://omahamagazine.com/articles/historic-buildings-of-the-old-market/

DENVER, COLORADO

Jaffe, Mark. "Denver's Renovated Union Station has been a 30-year Barn-raising." *Denver Post*, July 14, 2014. https://www.denverpost.com/2014/07/12/denvers-renovated-union-station-has-been-a-30-year-barn-raising/

McMahon, Edward T. "From Skid Row to LoDo: Historic Preservation's Role in Denver's Revitalization." *Urbanland*, October 11, 2012. https://urbanland.uli.org/development-business/from-skid-row-to-lodo-historic-preservation-s-role-in-denver-s-revitalization/

Seppanen, Jahla. "A Look at Il Posto's Illuminating Atmosphere." *Modern in Denver*, April 10, 2017. https://www.modernindenver.com/2017/04/a-look-at-il-postos-illuminating-atmosphere/

Sukin, Gigi. "The Denver Central Market and the Rise of the Food Hall." *Confluence Denver*, March 1, 2017. https://www.confluence-denver.com/features/denver-central-market-030117.aspx

Yuan, Jada. "The 52 Places Traveler: In Denver, a Mile High but Down to Earth." *New York Times*, May 15, 2018. https://www.nytimes.com/2018/05/15/travel/denver-food-art-outdoors-52-places.html

AUSTIN, TEXAS

de Monchaux, Thomas. 'Keep Austin Adaptive." *Architect*, June 6, 2011. https://www.architectmagazine.com/design/keep-austin-adaptive_o

Fazzare, Elizabeth. "Austin." *Architectural Digest*, April 30, 2018. https://www.architecturaldigest.com/story/austin

Keane, Katharine. "AIA 2017 Small Project Award Program Winners." *Architect*, June 23, 2017. https://www.architectmagazine.com/awards/aia-2017-small-project-award-program-winners_o

Murphy, Jack. "Austin's New Public Library Reflects the City's Transformation and Energy." *Architect's Newspaper,* February 16, 2018. https://archpaper.com/2018/02/austin-new-public-library-anchor-downtown-transformation/

Netze, Jaime. "Garage, Style in Austin." *Tribeza*, (n.d.). https://tribeza.com/style-pick-garage/

MARFA, TEXAS

Hall, Michael. "The Buzz About Marfa Is Just Crazy." *Texas Monthly*, August 31, 2004. https://www.texasmonthly.com/travel/the-buzz-about-marfa-is-just-crazy/

ENDPAGES A detail of the rusted architecture at Buffalo's RiverWorks.

PAGE 1 Iconic grain silos in Buffalo, New York, are repurposed as a climbing wall.

PAGE 2 In Richmond, Virginia, remnants of an old electric plant were transformed into an outdoor art gallery.

Editor: Rebecca Kaplan
Designer: Danielle Youngsmith
Production Manager: Kathleen Gaffney

Library of Congress Control Number: 2019936962

ISBN: 978-1-4197-3822-7
eISBN: 978-1-68335-874-9

Text copyright © 2020 Michel Arnaud
Introduction copyright © 2020 Donald Albrecht
Photographs copyright © 2020 Michel Arnaud
Page 191: Courtesy of the Mattress Factory
Page 244–245: Blanton Museum of Art, The University of Texas at Austin, Gift of the artist, with funding generously provided by Jeanne and Michael Klein, Judy and Charles Tate, the Scurlock Foundation, Suzanne Deal Booth and David G. Booth, the Longhorn Network, and other donors. © Ellsworth Kelly Foundation.

Cover © 2020 Abrams

Published in 2020 by Abrams, an imprint of ABRAMS. All rights reserved. No portion of this book may be reproduced, stored in a retrieval system, or transmitted in any form or by any means, mechanical, electronic, photocopying, recording, or otherwise, without written permission from the publisher.

Printed and bound in China
10 9 8 7 6 5 4 3 2 1

Abrams books are available at special discounts when purchased in quantity for premiums and promotions as well as fundraising or educational use. Special editions can also be created to specification. For details, contact specialsales@abramsbooks.com or the address below.

Abrams® is a registered trademark of
Harry N. Abrams, Inc.

ABRAMS The Art of Books
195 Broadway, New York, NY 10007
abramsbooks.com

ACKNOWLEDGMENTS

I would like to dedicate this book to my wife, Jane. Without her enthusiasm, support, and inspiration, this project would still be a dream.

A very special thanks to my editor, Rebecca Kaplan, who believed in this project from the start and has been unfailingly supportive. Thank you to the team at Abrams Books: Michael Sand, who directed us to North Adams; Deb Wood; and Danielle Youngsmith for her smart design.

It was an honor collaborating with Donald Albrecht who framed the story in a very insightful way and who gave us some invaluable contacts.

The warmest of thanks to the people who welcomed us into their homes, studios, or businesses, their participation, cooperation, enthusiasm, leads, and suggestions kept us going. And special thanks to those who educated us on each city: Brooks Williams and Christine Sullivan on Austin and Marfa, Texas; Sissy Austin Bishop on Birmingham; Steven Schwartz on Buffalo; Sara Sartarelli, Preeti Thakar, Judith and Shinji Turner-Yamamoto, and Keri Witman on Cincinnati; Stephen Brockman and Grunner Burke on Buffalo and Cincinnati; Jeff Dolezal and Maria Fernandez on Omaha; Sonya Cheng on Nashville; Melanie Abrantes, Evelyne Jouanno, and Andrew Collins on Oakland; Ingrid Schaffner on Pittsburgh; Jim Spivey on Portland; Robert Hicks, Ellen Jones Pryor, and Libby Callaway on Nashville; and Forrest Frazier, Beth O'Neill, Chris McVoy, and Isaac Regelson on Richmond.

In addition, thank you to our colleagues, friends, and family who provided us with ideas, assistance, and encouragement, in particular: Jeannie Avent, Nora Calderwood, Debra Castellano, Warren and Lenny Collins, Tom and Jane Creech, Tommy and Andrea Creech, Barbara Hogenson, Robin Osler, Nena Stone, Lori Styler, Holly Sumner, and Kimberly Sweet.

Lastly, I would like to thank my son Will for always being ready and helping whenever possible.

—Michel Arnaud, October 2019